THE STORY
OF GENERAL PERSHING

General Pershing.

THE STORY OF
GENERAL PERSHING

BY

EVERETT T. TOMLINSON

AUTHOR OF "FIGHTERS YOUNG AMERICANS WANT TO KNOW," ETC.

ILLUSTRATED

D. APPLETON AND COMPANY

NEW YORK   LONDON

1919

Printed in the United States of America

ACKNOWLEDGMENTS

THE writer gratefully acknowledges the aid he has received in the preparation of this book. To President Greene and Mr. J. E. Bell of William Jewell College, Missouri, he is under special obligations. Mr. Bell in order to aid the writer spent several days in Linn County, Missouri, verifying and obtaining facts. To Mr. Herbert Putnam of the Library of Congress, Mr. John Cotton Dana of the Newark, New Jersey, Public Library, and to Dr. Arthur E. Bostwick of the St. Louis Public Library he owes a special debt of gratitude for bibliographies and carefully prepared suggestions as to sources of information. From Cashin's "Under Fire with the 10th U. S. Cavalry," Missouri State Historical Review, Reports of the War Department and other publications, selections and citations have been made and from the facts contained in dispatches from France, particularly the very excellent reports in the New York *Times* and New York *Sun,* the writer has obtained valuable information. The direct aid of United States Senator Frelinghuysen in obtaining data from the War Department and the suggestion of United States Senator Warren have been most helpful. Replies to questions sent to friends and relatives of the General have assisted in verifying certain facts and figures. Many who personally knew the great commander in his younger days have very kindly given the writer such help as lay within their power. He gladly recognizes his indebtedness, especially to the following persons: Mr. Charles Spurgeon, Brookfield, Mo.; Judge O. F. Libby, Bigger, Mo.; H. C. Lomax, Esq., Laclede, Mo.; S. E. Carothers, Waco, Tex.; Mr. Robert S. Huse, Elizabeth, N. J., whose father was the "splendid old Caleb" of the Highland Military Academy; Hon. E. W. Stephens, Columbia, Mo.; Mrs. Louisa D. Warren, Meadville, Mo., and Mr. Wesley L. Love, Brookfield, Mo. Major James E. Runcie, Librarian of the United States Military Academy, West Point, N. Y., and General

P. C. Harris, acting the Adjutant General, have both been exceedingly kind in providing and verifying certain items of information which otherwise it would have been difficult if not impossible to obtain. The writer wishes to thank all these good people who have helped to make even the gathering of data an inspiration. Articles appearing in many current magazines and newspapers have provided interesting items, but the writer has quoted from them only after verification of certain details.

PREFACE

THE purpose of the writer of this little book is merely to tell the story in outline of the career of the commander of the American Expeditionary Forces in France. The modesty of General Pershing has kept his name out of print to a greater extent than in the case of many of our prominent men. His advancement also came rapidly in these recent years. As a result of these two conditions many of the fellow countrymen of the General are not familiar with the story of his early life or his successful work in the Philippines. This they not only have a right to know, but they ought to know.

The writer has endeavored to tell the story briefly as it has been told him, or as it has been kept in the records of the War Department and elsewhere. The complete biography and the analysis of General Pershing's personality and military career he leaves to later writers. The simple story of the struggles and achievements of a more or less typically successful American is presented, with the hope that others also may find in the record the inspiration and interest which the writer has found. Sometimes fighting against obstacles that appeared almost insurmountable, struggling to obtain an education in the schools, not faltering when tragic sorrows came, his determination succeeding in military campaigns where previous centuries of fighting had failed—the career of General Pershing has been a continuous overcoming. Confidence in a great leader is an essential condition of victory and the writer has tried to present facts to show that the trust of the American people in their military leader is well founded.

Some years ago a certain tight-fisted denizen of the United States inquired sneeringly of a young man from his village, who was working his way through college, "What do you expect to make of yourself anyway?" Instantly came the reply, "A man." Cause and effect, aim and incentive, object and motive alike are all summed up in that response. Behind the General is the man whose story the writer has tried to tell just as he has found it.

CONTENTS

LIST OF ILLUSTRATIONS

THE
STORY OF GENERAL PERSHING

CHAPTER I

A Historic Moment

THE morning of June 13, 1917, was one of the historic mornings in the history of the world. On the landing dock at Boulogne, France, a detachment of French infantry was drawn up in line. The men were clad in the uniform of battle. Their faces confirmed the report that recently they had seen hard service in the trenches—as they had. Not a young soldier was in the lines—they were all middle-aged men, perhaps made older by the fearful experiences through which they recently had passed.

1

This morning, however, there was an air of eagerness and expectancy in the expressions on their faces; and the eyes of all, with an intentness that was at once pathetic and tragic, were watching a boat that was drawing near the landing stage.

In the assembly on the dock an observer would have seen certain of the great men of France. There were Brigadier General Pelletier; René Bernard, Under Secretary of State for War; General Dumas; General Dupon, representing General Petain; and the military governor of Boulogne. Representatives of other nations and forces also were in the midst of the eager throng. There, too, were Sir George Fowke, representing General Sir Douglas Haig; and Captain Boyd, Military Attaché of the American War Department. Men, resplendent in their uniforms and decorations, who represented the British and French navies, also were in the assembly, all as deeply interested as were their military comrades. The nearby streets were filled with people waiting and subdued, and yet in a state of mind that at any

2

moment would have carried the great assembly into the wildest enthusiasm.

The cause of the excitement was to be found in a little group of men assembled on the deck of a steamer that was slowly approaching the dock. In the center of the group stood a man in the uniform of the United States Army. He was six feet in height, broad shouldered, trim-waisted, muscular and wiry. His hair was gray and his closely cropped mustache was also tinged with gray. His dark eyes were glowing, though every nerve and muscle was under the control of his will—a will that was as strong as his prominent chin and nose indicated. It was the first time in the history of the world that an American soldier was landing in Europe, there to fight for his own country and for the liberty of the world. There is slight cause for wonder that a murmur ran from one to another in the expectant crowd: "Truly here comes a man!" And the man was to be followed by millions, clad in the uniform of the land from which he came.

We may be sure that when this soldier, General John Joseph Pershing, stepped ashore and General Dumas greeted the American in the words, "I salute the United States of America, which has now become united to the United States of Europe," there was a cause for the deep emotion that manifested itself in Pershing's dark eyes. It was, as he said, "a historic moment." As he greeted the French colors, the detachment of brave men that had recently come from the firing line stood immovable like men of steel, and the American general slowly passed down the line, his face alone still betraying his feeling over the deep solemnity of the moment. And what a moment it was! Their dead had not died in vain, their heroic struggle against barbarism, all the sorrows and losses the devoted French people had borne were now focused on the coming of an American general and his staff. For behind him was America, and she was coming too.

And this American general, with his staff of fifty-three officers and one hundred and forty-six men, including privates and civilian attaches, stood before the beholders as the fore-

4

runners of a mighty host which was determined to help clear the world of the German menace to life, liberty and the pursuit of happiness. General Pershing, the fifth full general of the United States, is the successor to Washington, Grant, Sherman and Sheridan. So modest has been his career, so great his reluctance to appear in print, that many, even in his own nation, are not familiar with the deeds he has done. He has not sought promotion, but promotion sought him. Apparently, at times, in far away provinces, he has been banished to obscurity. Seven years passed before he was raised from the rank of a second lieutenant to a first lieutenancy, and yet the year 1917 found him in command of the American Expeditionary Forces in France, the first leader of American troops to land with drawn swords on the soil of Europe. The record is marvelous and it is also inspiring. What manner of man is this commander? What is the story of his life? Who were his father and mother? Where did he come from? How did he develop the powers that led one American

President to advance him eight hundred and sixty-two points at one time and caused another President to select him as the one man to command the soldiers of the United States in France? What are his qualifications—mental, moral and physical?

This story is an attempt to answer these questions in such a manner that the people of his own land may be able to understand a part at least of the career of the man behind the general. It does not try to analyze critically the military career of General John Joseph Pershing, nor does it primarily portray the development of the soldier. It is rather a modest recital of the leading events in the life of Pershing, the man, who became Pershing, the General.

CHAPTER II

Birth and Early Home

From this, the time of our greatest war, we must drop back approximately half a century to the time of our second greatest war. It is noteworthy that General Pershing, our leader in the war for the world's freedom, was born in the early days in the war for the negroes' freedom.

The future general first saw the light September 13, 1860, in or near the little village of Laclede, Missouri. The lad was "from Missouri" and the current semi-slang expression has certainly been true in his case. One had to "show him," for he made up his mind, mapped out his own plans and conducted his own studies and investigations. This characteristic has remained with him to this day. The accepted date of his birth and the house in which he was born are still matters of mild dispute among the good people of the little village of Laclede. A friend of his boyhood days says, "He was born in a section house about 3,000 yards from the site of the old depot. The foundation is still there." But the people of Laclede and Meadville, a nearby hamlet, are not a unit in this detail, though all are heartily agreed and proud in their recollection of the lad who since has made the little hamlet famous.

"Grandma" Warren (Mrs. Louisa D.) through her daughter sends the following contribution to this mooted question:

"My mother states that in the spring of 1859, the General's father and mother, then recently married, came to board with her father, Meredith Brown, who resided about two and one-half miles east of Meadville, Mo. My mother, then a widow, was living at the home of her father and was associated with the Pershings that summer.

"In the fall of the year the Pershings moved to a house of their own about a half mile west of the Brown home and this is the place where the General was born. The tract of land on which the house stood is now owned by John Templeman and is the north $\frac{1}{2}$ of Sec. 5, T'wp 57, range 21, Linn Co., Mo. The house in which the General was born was destroyed by fire during the Civil War. Mother was present at the General's birth and dressed him in his first suit.

"From the house where the General was born they moved to what was known as the 'Section House,'— a house built for the section foreman of the railroad. This house was located about two miles west of Meadville on the Hannibal and St. Joseph R. R., now the Burlington.

"During the time from 1859 and a few years later, the senior Pershing was section foreman on this road. At the last mentioned place of residence the second child was born.

"After a few years' residence at the section house, the family moved to Laclede, Mo., seven miles east of Meadville. At this place the father engaged in mercantile business, continuing in the business for a number of years. My mother visited at the Pershing home at this place frequently. After leaving Laclede, mother lost communication with them.

"The citizens of Meadville and vicinity have in the course of construction at the present time a large sign to be erected at the birthplace of the General. My mother is now in her 85th year.

"The place of the General's birth is near a small stream known as Hickory Branch and the community along this stream is known as the Hickory Branch Community. In closing, I wish to pay my respects to the General: John J. Pershing, the baby, belongs to

Hickory Branch. John J. Pershing, the man, belongs to the world.

"Yours truly,

"E. S. WARREN."

It is not strange if seven cities contended with one another for the honor of being the birthplace of Homer that two small villages in Missouri are divided in their claims for a similar honor in the case of the present foremost American soldier. As to the merits of the contest it is impossible to pronounce judgment at this time. The General himself has only hearsay evidence of the exact locality of his birth, though there is no question as to its having taken place in Linn County, Missouri, and that his boyhood was passed in the village of Laclede.

The General's father, John F. Pershing, a short time before the birth of his oldest child (the general), came from Westmoreland County, Pennsylvania, and went to work as a section foreman on the Hannibal and St. Joe Railroad. He was a forceful man, of energy and ambition, and it was not long before he

10

The Home of the Pershings, Laclede, Missouri.

was running a general store and at the same time was postmaster of the village. A man now living, who worked for the General's father in both the general store and post office, has this tribute to pay to his one time employer: ¶He was a very active business man with wonderful energy, strictly honest, never stooped to a dishonest trick; a pronounced man in the community; the leading business man. He liked to make money. He lost two fortunes on the Board of Trade, Chicago. He traveled several years out of St. Joseph, probably one of the best paid men. He later left St. Joe for Chicago, where he was traveling salesman for another firm. He made many business ventures —was something of what to-day is called a promoter.

"He was a man of commanding presence. He was a great family man, loved his family devotedly. He was not lax and ruled his household well."

The older Pershing was insistent that his children should be able to meet the difficulties in life that must be overcome before success can be won. The value of regular habits of appreciation of the things worth while, was his hobby and he taught by example as well as by precept. Hard work was essential. Therefore hard work must be undertaken and done, and he began early to train his three boys and three girls, who of the nine that were born to him grew to maturity. His creed included the precept that it is well to learn to bear the yoke in one's youth. Every Sunday the Pershing family were seen on their way to the little Methodist church of which the father and mother were members, Mr. Pershing at one time being superintendent of the Sunday School. He is reported also to have been a local preacher. He was one of the founders of his church.

A neighbor writes, "When the Civil War broke out, the elder Pershing left the railroad and became the regimental sutler of the old 18th Mo. Reg. Infantry. Later he engaged in merchandising and farming with success, but was caught in the panic of 1873. About 1876, he went to work for I. Weil & Company of St. Joseph, Mo., as a traveling salesman, selling clothing, and later for a big Chicago house. The family lived at Laclede until about 1886, at which time they moved to Lincoln, Nebraska, where two of the daughters now reside. General Pershing's father and mother are both dead.

"The Pershing family were zealous church people. John F. Pershing was the Sunday School superintendent of the Methodist Church all the years he lived here, I think, or until he commenced to work for I. Weil & Co. Every Sunday you could see him making his way to church with John (the general) on one side and Jim on the other, Mrs. Pershing and the little girls following along. The family was a serious loss to the Methodist church when they moved away from here."

Throughout his life there was an air of seriousness under which the future general was brought up. Doubtless from his earliest days the impression that if he was to do anything worth while he must first be something worth while, consciously or unconsciously influenced

13

the life of the son of the father, who was eager to have his children secure the best education within their power to obtain and his ability to give. At all events, the General's life-plan seems to have been to get ready, whether or not the test comes. If it does come, one is prepared; if it does not come one is prepared just the same. Here again it was the man behind the general, shaped, guided, trained and inspired by the strong, earnest personality of his father.

From a member of the Pershing family the following statement has been received: "His (the general's) father was born near Pittsburgh, Pa., his ancestors having come from Alsace-Lorraine. He was prominent in church work and all philanthropic work. He established the Methodist Church at Laclede, Mo., and after moving to Chicago was instrumental in forming the Hyde Park Methodist Church. He was also active in the Y. M. C. A., Chicago, and organized the Hyde Park branch. He was in the Union Army and was the first man to observe Memorial Day in Laclede, taking his own children and the children of his neighborhood,

14

with flowers from his own garden, to decorate
the graves of the soldiers. Mr. Pershing (John
Fletcher Pershing) was president of the school
board at Laclede and it was through his work
that the graded schools were organized and
new buildings erected. He was also postmaster
in Laclede.''

Of his mother—the best report from Laclede
is that she was a "splendid home maker."
Why is it that most great men have had great
mothers? Frequently we are disappointed in
the sons of great men. Either the boys do not
measure up to their sires, or we are prone to
expect too much of them, or, as is quite likely,
we contrast the young man at the beginning of
his career with the reputation of his father
when it is at its zenith.

But history is filled with examples of men
who have attributed all they have done or won
to the inspiring love and devotion of the
mothers that bore them. And General Pershing
is no exception to this rule. One time, when,
after years of absence he came back to Laclede
as a brigadier general in the army of the

United States, he went to call upon Aunt Susan Hewett, an aged widow and old resident of the town. In his boyhood, Aunt Susan and her husband, "Captain" Hewett, had "run the hotel." Aunt Susan in her prime was famous for her pies and her love of boys, and Johnnie Pershing was a favorite. As a result of her affection for the lad he was a frequent and successful sampler of her wares. The picture of Aunt Susan and her pies and the sampling done by the future general of the United States Army is one that is easily imagined and strongly appeals to those who know the worth of well made pies,—for in spite of local pride, good pies are not all limited to New England.

To a reporter two or three years ago Aunt Susan said,* "Law, yes, I remember John when he wasn't more'n two or three years old. When John was big enough to put on trousers he used to eat more pies in our kitchen than any other boy in town.

"He was back here about ten years ago. It

*Missouri Historical Review.

was on the 24th day of October that Uncle Henry Lomax came to my house and said, 'Aunt Susan, there's a gentleman outside that wants to see you.' When I stepped outside and saw a tall young man, Uncle Henry asked me if I knew who it was.

" 'Yes,' I said, 'it's John Pershing. I can see his mother's features in his face.' He came to me with his arms open and he embraced me and kissed me and we both cried. 'Aunt Susan,' he says, and I'll never forget his words as long as I live, 'it does my heart good to see my mother's dear old friends. The place seems like home to me and it always will. I've been away a long time and there have been many changes, but this is home.' The chrysanthemums were in bloom and after we had talked a while in the parlor I went out and picked a bouquet for him to take away.

" 'They are going to have some kind of a reception for me to-night and I want you to come, Aunt Susan,' he says. I told him I'd try to be there but that I was tired and worn out because I had been working hard in the garden. 'You

17

won't have to walk, Aunt Susan, because I'll come after you myself.' About five in the afternoon he came in a buggy. We went to his reception together and my! what a crowd. The whole house was packed and people were standing in the yard. Johnny shook hands with everybody and talked to them and he finally made a speech, which I didn't hear because there were so many people around. John Pershing always did have talent.''

This incident of his later years is eloquent of the earlier years—and of Pershing's mother. Behind the figure of the living is another who being dead, yet speaketh. "A splendid home maker.''

The relatives of General Pershing disclaim all knowledge of this incident and are inclined to pronounce it "mostly fiction." The incident is taken from the *Missouri Historical Review.* In other forms also the story has become current. A former friend of the family, now a resident of Laclede, also questions the reliability of the tale, basing his conclusion upon the fact that the local village taverns were not places which such a man as General Pershing's father would knowingly permit his boys to frequent.

Nor is Aunt Susan's fact (or fiction) the only tribute. Before me is a letter from a long time friend and neighbor of the family which states: "Mrs. Pershing stood high among her neighbors. She was a woman of unusual intelligence and much better educated than the average woman of those days. She was an unusually cultivated woman. Mr. Pershing probably had the best library in the town. His father and mother were both religious and John went to Sunday School and church every Sunday." The deep affection is apparent as one reads between the lines of many letters received from those who years ago knew her both personally and well. It is not difficult to trace the source of the inspiration of Pershing's life.

An intimate friend of the General in response to a personal request has courteously given the following modest statement: "General Pershing's mother was Ann Elizabeth Thompson. She was born near Nashville, Tenn. Although she came of a southern family she joined her husband in her sympathy for the cause of the North, and made the first flag that was raised in Linn County, thereby risking the lives of her family. One of her brothers was in the Southern army, and one served on the Northern side. When her brother, Colonel L. A. Thompson, was wounded, her husband secured permission to cross the line and brought him home. Mrs. Pershing was always an inspiration for her children and her ambition for them, especially in an educational way, was without bounds.''

And there came a time when General Pershing doubtless realized as never before all that his mother had been to him. His troops were mounted and he was about to give the command for the departure of his men on an expedition against the Moros. At that moment an orderly advanced and gave him a message which informed him of the death of his mother, in her far away home. It was a blow as hard as it was sudden. The face of the leader was almost ghastly in its whiteness. He swallowed hard two or three times and then quietly gave the command for his troops to advance. He was a soldier of his country and the message which had brought him the deepest sorrow of his life up to that time must not be permitted to allow his personal grief to interfere with his duty. The lesson his mother had taught him was put to the test and was not forgotten.

CHAPTER III

Boyhood and Student Days

In the family were three boys and three girls (of the nine children) that lived to manhood and womanhood. Ward, the general's younger brother, an officer in the Spanish-American war, is dead. Lieutenant Paddock married the General's sister, Grace. He died in China during the Boxer uprising. Two other sisters now reside in Lincoln and a brother is in business in Chicago.

The writer quoted above also says, "John was always settled as a boy. There was nothing sensational or spectacular about him. He had the confidence of everybody." Another of his boyhood chums writes: "John Pershing was a clean, straight, well behaved young fellow. He never was permitted to loaf around on the streets. Nobody jumped on him and he didn't

General Pershing as a Boy.

jump on anybody. He attended strictly to his own business. He had his lessons when he went to class. He was not a big talker. He said a lot in a few words, and didn't try to cut any swell. He was a hard student. He was not brilliant, but firm, solid and would hang on to the very last. We used to study our lessons together evenings. About nine-thirty or ten o'clock, I'd say:

"'John, how are you coming?'

"'Pretty stubborn.'

"'Better go to bed, hadn't we?'

"'No, Charley, I'm going to work this out.'"

One, who distinctly recalls him as a boy, describes him: "His hair was light and curly. He had large black eyes; was square-jawed and was iron-willed. His shoulders were square, and he was straight as an arrow. He had a firm, set mouth and a high forehead, and even as a boy was a dignified chap. And yet he was thoroughly democratic in his manner and belief."

Another, who was a playmate, has the following tribute: "As a boy Pershing was not unlike thousands of other boys of his age, enjoying the same pleasures and games as his other boyhood companions. He knew the best places to shoot squirrels or quail, knew where to find the hazel or hickory nuts. He knew, too, where the coolest and deepest swimming pools in the Locust, Muddy or Turkey creeks were. Many a time we went swimming together in Pratt's pond. At school John was studious and better able than the most of us to grasp the principles outlined in the text books. As a rule he led his classes, particularly in mathematics. His primary education was obtained in a little white school house of one room, eighteen by twenty feet, which is still standing. Later he attended Lewis Hall, a building which formerly was a hospital in the War of the Rebellion. It was located across the street from the Pershing residence. This building later was moved to the old Pershing farm (now owned by Mrs. John Deninger's family) and is used as a barn.

"John was and is naturally human and that

is why he always had so many friends. His old playmates and friends are all proud of his success as a soldier, but they love him because of his high standards of principles and his unswerving integrity. As a boy he was forceful, honest in every way and when he had given his word we all knew we could depend upon it absolutely."

This boyhood friend acknowledges modestly that he and John were not entirely ignorant of the sensations produced by certain hickory or osage switches in the hands of an irate or hasty teacher, but this chapter is not enlarged. There is, however, an unconsciously proud and tender touch in his closing words, "I have two sons in the army doing their bit, and I am thankful that they will be under the direction and order of my old friend, John J. Pershing." True praise could not be better expressed than in this gracious and kindly reference.

But the future general's boyhood was not all, nor even chiefly devoted to swimming and nutting. There was hard work to be done and he was a hard worker. Long rows of corn had to be planted and cultivated, pigs and cattle must be fed and cared for, and the "chores" on a Missouri farm began early in the morning and were not all done when at last the sun set. The boy Pershing did much of his labor on the farms that his father had leased near the village. Frequently the farm-work lasted until late in the fall and thereby interfered with attendance at school. Here, too, there were obstacles to be overcome and the commander of our army in France was early learning his lessons of control and self-control in a little hamlet in Missouri.

At that time Laclede and vicinity had more negroes than whites in its population. When Pershing had arrived at the mature age of seventeen, the teacher of a local negro school suddenly left and the school was turned over to him. There were three elements in the "call" to this untried position—the school had no other teacher, the need was great and in spite of his youthfulness it was believed there was no one who could do better under the circumstances for the colored children than he.

26

He understood them, he wanted to help them, and he was able to control them. And he did. "Discipline," as it was commonly understood in the country schools, might have been defined as the ability to whip the older boys. Discipline as a positive as well as a negative force was something new, and the new teacher finished the year with the reputation of having trained his pupils to do something worth while.

Then white schools were taken by the youthful pedagogue, and in them also he succeeded. There was growing up in his mind a strong determination to secure an education. In this way he was earning and saving money by which he should be able to carry out his growing plans. Dimly in the background also was an ambition ultimately to study law. In this desire not only his father and mother but also his sister now was sharing.

In the *Missouri Historical Record,* April-July, 1917, there is recorded the story of a contest into which the young teacher was forced by an irate farmer whose children had been disciplined.

"Though he never sought a quarrel, young Pershing was known even at this time among his fellows as a 'game fighter,' who never acknowledged defeat. To a reporter for the *Kansas City Star,* who was a pupil under Pershing when the general was a country school teacher at Prairie Mound, thirty-seven years ago, was recently related an incident of him as a fighting young schoolmaster. One day at the noon hour a big farmer with red sideburns rode up to the schoolhouse with a revolver in his hand. Pershing had whipped one of the farmer's children and the enraged parent intended to give the young schoolmaster a flogging.

"I remember how he rode up cursing before all the children in the schoolyard and how another boy and I ran down a gully because we were afraid. We peeked over the edge, though, and heard Pershing tell the farmer to put up his gun, get down off his horse and fight like a man.

"The farmer got down and John stripped off his coat. He was only a boy of seventeen or eighteen and slender, but he thrashed the old

28

The Church the Pershings attended at
Laclede.

The Prairie Mound School.

farmer soundly. And I have hated red side-burns ever since.''

Through all these various experiences he was saving every penny possible, with the thought in view of the education he was determined to obtain. At last the time arrived when he and his sister departed for Kirksville, Mo., to enter the State Normal School. His father had done all in his power for him, but his main reliance now was upon himself. There he continued his former steady methodical methods, doing well, but not being looked upon as an exceptionally brilliant student. He was still the same persistent, reliable, hard-working, successful student he had formerly been.

It is not quite clear just when his decision for West Point was made. His room-mate at the State Normal School reports that it was in the spring when he and Pershing were at home in vacation time that the matter was decided. According to his recollection and report to the writer, when the two boys were at home the elder Pershing urged his son's room-mate again to enter his store as clerk. A definite answer was postponed until the following day. "So next day I saw Pershing," he writes, "and asked him what he was going to do. He didn't know; he didn't want to teach a spring term of school; believed he would go back to Kirksville for ten weeks. And then came the West Point opportunity."

Another friend of Pershing at that time sends the following quotation from the local paper which evidently places the date at another time: "In looking over some old papers the other day, I ran across a copy of the *Laclede News* under date of December 28th, 1881, and among other news items found the following: 'John J. Pershing will take his leave of home and friends this week for West Point, where he will enter the United States Military Academy. John will make a first-rate good-looking cadet with Uncle Sam's blue, and we trust he will ever wear it with honor to himself and the old flag which floats above him. John, here's our hand! May success crown your efforts and long life be yours.' "

In reality, however, the only confusion is between the time when the thought entered Pershing's mind and the time when he entered the Military Academy.

An advertisement had appeared in the local papers concerning a competitive examination for entrance. The announcement bore the name of Congressman J. H. Barrows, the "greenback" representative of the district, formerly a Baptist minister. He was looked upon by his constituency as true and reliable, a reputation that was not without its appeal to the lads who wanted to go to West Point. It is a current report that not always had these appointments been made on merit alone and that "from $250 to $500 was the amount frequently paid to obtain them." The examination was to be conducted at Trenton, Mo., and was open to all who were eligible.

Pershing decided to try. In making this decision his sister strongly encouraged him, and was the only one of his family who was aware of his plan. His room-mate writes that Pershing urged him also to try. "No," I told him, "I didn't know that I could pass." "Well," he said, "you'd better come and we'll take a chance. One or the other of us ought to win." I told him he had been in school three months while I had been selling goods, and that if he thought he would like it, to go, that I didn't care for it. But I should like to have the education, though I should probably stay in the army if I happened to pass. "No," he said, "I wouldn't stay in the army. There won't be a gun fired in the world for a hundred years. If there isn't, I'll study law, I guess, but I want an education and now I see how I can get it."

Eighteen took the examination and Pershing won, though by only a single point, and that was given only after he and his competitor, Higginbottom, had broken the tie by each diagraming the following sentence—"*I love to run!*"

Higginbottom's solution—

"I"—subject.

"love"—predicate.

"to run"—infinitive phrase qualifying the meaning of the verb.

Pershing's solution was as follows:

"I"—subject.

"love"—predicate.

"to run"—is the object.

The commission preferred Pershing's diagram, and thus by a single point he won the competitive examination and received the appointment.

When, however, Pershing and his sister informed their mother that he had passed the best examination and was to receive the appointment to West Point, she expressed her strong disapproval of the plan to make a soldier of John. Her objections were finally overcome, and she consented, partly because she believed her boy when he said "there would not be a gun fired for a hundred years" and partly because she was even more eager than he for him to obtain a good education.

Thirty years afterward General Pershing himself wrote: "The proudest days of my life, with one exception, have come to me in connection with West Point days that stand out clear and distinct from all others. The first of these

33

was the day I won my appointment at Trenton, Missouri, in a competitive examination with seventeen competitors. An old friend of the family happened to be at Trenton that day and passing on the opposite side of the street called to me and said, 'John, I hear you passed with flying colors.' In all seriousness, feeling the great importance of my success, I naively replied in a loud voice, 'Yes, I did,' feeling assured that no one had ever passed such a fine examination as I had.''

In spite of his success, however, Pershing was not yet ready to take up the strenuous course in the Military Academy. The work is severe and only the fittest are supposed to survive. He must have a more careful preparation in certain branches, he decided, and accordingly entered the Highland Military Academy, Highland Falls, New York, in which he continued as a student until the following June (1882). The head of the school was sincerely loved and deeply respected by his boys, and in after years General Pershing usually referred to him as "splendid old Caleb"—for

The Highland Military Academy.

United States Military Academy, West Point, N. Y.

"Caleb" was the title the students had bestowed upon Col. Huse.

In the military school Pershing's record is much what one who has followed his development in the preceding years would expect it to be. He was an earnest, consistent student, doing well and steadily improving in his work, without any flashes of brilliancy. He was moving not by leaps but steadily toward the education he was determined to obtain.

Those who recall him as a pupil at Highland say that he is best remembered for his physical strength and his skill as a horseman. Doubtless he had had training and experiences which were outside those which many of his classmates had shared.

At last in July, 1882, when he was not quite twenty-two years of age, Pershing became a plebe in the United States Military Academy at West Point. A part of his dream had been realized. His record shows that he still was manifesting the traits he already had displayed. Persistent, determined, methodical, a hard and steady worker, he was numbered thirty when he graduated in his class of seventy-seven. However, his "all around" qualities were shown by the fact that in his fourth class or final year, upon the recommendation of the commandant of Cadets, he was appointed by the Superintendent of the Academy to be the senior, that is, first in rank, of all the cadet captains—an honor worth while and of which Pershing was justly proud.

His love of West Point has always been strong. He is proud of the school and proud to be counted among its graduates. Loyal in all ways he has been specially loyal to West Point. Perhaps his true feeling can be best shown by the following letter written by him when he was in far-away Mindanao. He was class president at the time and sent the letter for the twenty-fifth anniversary of the graduation of the class. Like many an "old grad" the thoughts of the writer turn affectionately to the old days. The joys and disappointments are alike remembered and General Pershing shows a slight tendency to recall an occasional slip in the strict rules of the institution. This infraction is not upheld by him, and his friends, who are fully aware of his belief in strict discipline, will perhaps condone the slight infringement when they are aware that he records also the strict penalty which followed it. He indirectly shows that the infraction was due not to a desire to avoid a task but came of a grim determination to accomplish it.

GREETING TO THE CLASS.

Headquarters, Department of Mindanao.
Zamboanga, P. I.
March 15, 1911.

To the Class of 1886,
U. S. Military Academy,
West Point, New York.

DEAR CLASSMATES:

The announcement in the circular sent out by your committee saying that I would write a letter of greeting to be read at the class reunion imposes upon me a very pleasant obligation. It gives me an opportunity as Class President to write you collectively and to say many things that I would like to say if I were writing to each individual. Above all, however, I am permitted to feel myself a real part of the reunion. This letter shall be a heartfelt and sincere word of greeting from the opposite side of the world. I shall try to imagine myself among you around the banquet table or perhaps again in the old tower room, first floor, first division, or familiarly even in the "usual place." With this greeting I also send a word of explanation and regret for my absence, a few lines of reminiscence and pages of affection and friendship for all recorded at random.

It is unfortunate indeed for me that higher authority has concluded that I should not leave my post at this time. This is a great disappointment to me. There is nothing that could equal the pleasure of meeting once more with old '86—companions of my youth, the friendship for whom is above all others the dearest and most lasting. To be again for a few hours as in the olden days at West Point with those who stood shoulder to shoulder with me and I with them through over four years, would be worth a great sacrifice. The thought makes me long for cadet days again. I would gladly go back into the corps (although of course it has gone entirely to the dogs since we were cadets) and gladly (in spite of this) go through the whole course from beginning to end to be with you all as we were then. Life meant so much to us—probably more than it ever has since—when the soul was filled to the utmost with ambition and the world was full of promise.

The proudest days of my life, with one exception, have come to me in connection with West Point days that stand out clear and distinct from all others. The first of these was the day I won my appointment at Trenton, Missouri, in a competitive examination with seventeen competitors. An old friend of the family happened to be at Trenton that day and passing on the opposite side of the street, called to me and said, "John, I hear you passed with flying colors." In all seriousness, feeling the great importance of my success, I naively replied, in a loud voice, "Yes, I did," feeling assured that no one had ever quite passed such a fine examination as I had. The next red letter day was when I was elected President of the Class of '86. I didn't know much about class presidents until the evening of our meeting to effect a class organization. To realize that a body of men for whom I had such an affectionate regard should honor me in this way was about all my equilibrium would stand. Another important day was when I made a cold max in Phil. at June examination under dear old Pete, with Arthur Murray as instructor. This was the only max I ever made in anything. I fairly floated out of the library and back to the barracks. The climax of days came when the marks were read out on graduation day in June, 1886. Little Eddy Gayle smiled when I reported five minutes later with a pair of captain's chevrons pinned on my sleeves. No honor has ever come equal to that. I look upon it in the very same light to-day as I did then. Some way these days stand out and the recollection of them has always been to me a great spur and stimulus.

What memories come rushing forward to be recorded. It was at Colonel Huse's school, now called The Rocks, I believe, with splendid old Caleb at its head that several of us got the first idea of what we were really in for. Deshon, Frier, Winn, Andrews, Clayton, Billy Wright, Stevens, Segare and the rest of us at Caleb's used to wrestle with examinations of previous years and flyspeck page after page of stuff that we forgot completely before Plebe camp was over.

This brings up a period of West Point life whose vivid impressions will be the last to fade. Marching into camp, piling bedding, policing company streets for logs or wood carelessly dropped by upper classmen, pillow fights at tattoo with Marcus Miller, sabre drawn marching up and down superintending the plebe class, policing up feathers from the general parade; light artillery drills, double timing around old Fort Clinton at morning squad drill, Wiley Bean and the sad fate of his seersucker coat; midnight dragging, and the whole summer full of events can only be mentioned in passing. No one can ever forget his first guard tour with all its preparation and perspiration. I got along all right during the day, but at night on the color line my troubles began. Of course, I was scared beyond the point of properly applying any of my orders. A few minutes after taps, ghosts of all sorts began to appear from all directions. I selected a particularly bold one and challenged according to orders, "Halt, who comes there?" At that the ghost stood still in its tracks.

Cal. Huse
"Splendid Old Caleb"

Kirksville, Mo., State Normal School.

I then said, "Halt, who stands there?" Whereupon the ghost, who was carrying a chair, sat down. When I promptly said, "Halt, who sits there?"

After plebe camp came plebe math and French. I never stood high in French and was prone to burn the midnight oil. One night Walcott and Burtley Mott came in to see me. My roommate, "Lucy" Hunt, was in bed asleep. Suddenly we heard Flaxy, who was officer in charge, coming up the stairs several steps at a time. Mott sprang across the hall into his own room. I snatched the blanket from the window, turned out the light and leaped into bed, clothing and all, while Walcott seeing escape impossible, gently woke Hunt, and in a whisper said, "Lucy, may I crawl under your bed?" I paid the penalty by walking six tours of extra duty.

The rest of it—yearling camp and its release from plebedom, the first appearance in the riding hall of the famous '86 New England Cavalry, furlough and the return up the Hudson on the *Mary Powell;* second year class with its increasing responsibilities and dignity—must all be passed with slight notice. While the days were not always filled with unalloyed pleasure, to be sure, yet no matter how distasteful anything else may have been up to that time there is none of us who would not gladly live first class camp over again—summer girls, summer hops, first class privileges, possible engagements, twenty-eighth hop, and then the home stretch. As we look back from the distance of a quarter of a century the years went by all too rapidly.

The career of '86 at West Point was in many respects remarkable. There were no cliques, no dissensions and personal prejudices or selfishness, if any existed, never came to the surface. From the very day we entered, the class as a unit has always stood for the very best traditions of West Point. The spirit of old West Point existed to a higher degree in the class of '86 than in any class since the war. The West Point under Merritt, Michie and Hasbrouck was still the West Point of Grant, Sherman, Sheridan, Schofield and Howard. The deep impression these great men made during their visits to West Point in our day went far to inspire us with the soldier's spirit of self-sacrifice, duty and honor. Those characteristics were carried with us into the Army and have marked the splendid career of the class during the past twenty-five years. The Class of '86 has always been known in the Army and is known to-day as a class of all-around solid men—capable of ably performing any duty and of loyally fulfilling any trust. The individual character of each man has made itself felt upon his fellows in the Army from the start. In civil life, as professional men, or as men of affairs, wherever placed the Class of '86 has always made good. Well may we congratulate ourselves upon reaching this quarter century milestone, on the achievements of the class.

If I thought you would listen longer I should continue, but the evening will be full of song and reminiscence. Those of us out here will assemble at Manila and wish we were with you at West Point. It may be that age and experience will prevent a repetition of the lurid scenes enacted at the class dinner in New York in '86. Yet when you feel time turn backward and the hot blood of those days again courses through your veins, there is no telling what may happen. Still all will be for the glory of the Class and will be condoned. Then here's to the Class of '86, wives and sweethearts, children and grandchildren, your health and your success!

Always affectionately,

J. J. P.

CHAPTER IV

FIGHTING THE APACHES AND THE SIOUX

AT last the days at West Point were ended and the class of '86 was to take its place with others in the wide, wide world. To young Pershing fell the lot to be assigned to the Sixth Cavalry in the southwest, where General Miles, the successor of General Crook, was soon to bring the war against the Apaches to an end. He was then a second lieutenant.

The wily and daring leader of the redmen was commonly known as Geronimo, a medicine man and prophet of the Chiricahuas. Strictly speaking, the Indian's true name was Goyath-lay, "one who yawns," but the Mexicans had nicknamed him Geronimo—the Spanish for Jerome.

This Indian was born about 1834, near the headquarters of the Gila River, in New Mexico.

He was the son of Taklishim, "The Gray One." Neither the father nor the son was a chief, although Geronimo's grandfather claimed to be a chieftain without having been born to the purple or elected by the tribe.

In 1876, the Mexican authorities complained bitterly to the United States of the raids and depredations in the state of Sonora by the Chiricahua Indians with the result that it was decided by the Government to remove the tribe from their reservation on the southern border, to San Carlos, Arizona. But Geronimo, who was a natural leader, soon gathered a few of the younger chiefs about him and fled into Mexico.

Later, he was arrested and sent with his band to Ojo Caliente, New Mexico. There, apparently, thoughts of war were abandoned and the redmen became successful tillers of the soil in the San Carlos Reservation.

After a time, the tribe once more became restless and discontented because the Government would not help them to irrigate their lands. Just how much justice was in the claim it is

45

impossible now to ascertain. Other nearby lands were being watered and this favoritism, as they believed, as well as the competition of the neighboring ranches, doubtless had a strong effect on the Indians. At all events, in 1882, Geronimo was the leader of a band that was engaged in many raids in Sonora, but at last his force was surrounded and he surrendered to General George H. Crook in the Sierra Madre.

In spite of the fact that Geronimo had one of the very best farms in the entire San Carlos Reservation, the Apache leader soon was again in trouble with the United States in 1884, when attempts were made to stop the making and sale of tiswin. This was an Indian drink and highly intoxicating.

In 1884-5, Geronimo gathered and led a band of Apaches that not only terrorized the settlers in southern Arizona and New Mexico, but also the inhabitants of Sonora and Chihuahua in Mexico. General Crook was ordered to proceed against the raiders and to capture or kill the chief and his followers. The story of the war is filled with exciting deeds of daring, but

The Lieutenant in the Family.

through them all Geronimo looms as the foremost figure. His name came to inspire terror.

At last in March, 1886, a truce was made and this was followed by a conference, at which terms of surrender were agreed upon. But the wily Geronimo was not yet caught. Again with a band of his devoted followers he fled to the Sierra Madre mountains, beyond the borders of Mexico.

General Miles was now in command of the United States troops and quickly he began an energetic campaign against the Apache outlaws. This continued until August, when the war came to an end. The entire band of 340 were made prisoners and the warfare at last was ended. Geronimo and Nachi (the latter a hereditary chieftain of the tribe, though his comrade was the real leader), were sent as prisoners of war to Florida. Later they were removed to Alabama and at last were settled near Fort Sill, Oklahoma. There, Geronimo evidently concluded (and his conclusion was the more easily arrived at because he was under the continual supervision of United States soldiers) that he had had a sufficiency of war and that henceforth he was to be a man of peace. He became prosperous, and was a most cautious spender of his money.

The part which Lieutenant Pershing, a young officer fresh from West Point, had in the round-up of this campaign naturally was not of a character to bring him into great prominence. That he did his work well and that he had the full confidence of his men, however, are evidenced from the following incidents which remain among the reports of the campaign.

In the autumn maneuver in 1887, he was specially complimented by General Miles for "marching his troops with a pack train of 140 mules in 46 hours and bringing in every animal in good condition." Doubtless his early experiences in dealing with mules on a Missouri farm had stood him in good stead.

Another instance of his courage and his ability to deal with men, even at this early stage in his career, was shown when word came of the dire predicament of a score of "bad men"—horse thieves and cow-punchers—who had been surrounded by the Indians and were threatened with the death of every one in the band unless they should be speedily rescued. The young lieutenant with his detachment not only succeeded in penetrating to their refuge, but also in saving every one of them without the loss of the life of one man, white or red. The same qualities that had been displayed in his student days were here again in evidence. His sense of duty was still strong upon him and quietly, persistently, he worked hard to do his best.

There still was work for the lieutenant on the border, for the troubles with the Indian tribes were by no means ended. His service on frontier duty at Fort Bayard, New Mexico, and in the field from July 30, 1886, to July 30, 1887, was followed by duty at Fort Stanton, New Mexico.

He went to Fort Wingate, New Mexico, in February, 1889, remaining there until September 1, 1889. He then returned to Fort Stanton to stay until September, 1890, when again he was sent to Fort Wingate.

At Fort Wingate, with the exception of a few weeks spent in scout duty, he remained until December 1, 1890, when he was transferred to take the field in the campaign against the Sioux Indians at Pine Ridge Agency, South Dakota. In February, 1891, he was stationed at Fort Niobrara, in Nebraska, only to return to the Pine Ridge Agency to take command of the Sioux Indian Scouts until July of the same year. Again he was with his troops at Fort Niobrara, remaining until August 7, 1891, when he was in command of a detachment (rifle team) en route to Fort Sheridan, Illinois. On September 25th he became Professor of Military Science and Tactics at the University of Nebraska at Lincoln, Nebraska.

This brief record, however, does not cover all that the young officer was doing. Studying and at the same time working hard at his duties, he was already laying the foundations for that which later was to come. At the time, however, his future career seemed vague if not impossible. Indeed, he himself was almost convinced that war had ceased to be a threat among the nations. "There won't be a gun fired in a hundred years," he had declared to a friend when he was about to enter West Point, and the thoughts of the young officer reverted to the law for which in his younger days he had almost decided to prepare.

That he was not without suggestions and desires to improve the conditions in the army is shown by the following letter which he wrote the *Journal of United States Cavalry* in 1889:

[Journal of U. S. Cavalry, December, 1889.]
Some Hints for Improvement.

More prominence should be given to the revolver competitions and some changes might be made in the manner of conducting them. We should have a regular revolver competition and teams with competitors one from each troop held every morning, best pistol shots in the troop, and not have pistol competition supplementary to carbine competition though the two might be held at the same time and place.

In connection with the army carbine competition there should be an army revolver, competitors to be selected from the various revolver teams as they are held for the army carbine competitions.

Prizes for the revolver teams should be the same as those awarded to the infantry department and for the army revolver team the same as those awarded to the infantry division teams.

No good reason can be seen why dismounted revolver firing should not be held at the three ranges, 25, 50 and 75 yards, the same as for individual record in the troop. In the mounted firing, both in troops and practice competitions, no gait slower than ten miles and a half should be permitted. These changes would give a stimulus to revolver firing in the army which would bring about surprising results.

J. J. PERSHING,
Second Lieutenant, 6th Cavalry.

In the part which Lieutenant Pershing took against the Sioux, he was sharing conditions which were by no means slight or insignificant. The Sioux were notably brave and bold and more than once their chiefs had outgeneraled the trained white soldiers that fought them.

It is difficult to determine at this time just where to place the blame for these wars with the Sioux. The stories of the causes of the outbreak told by the Indians themselves differ radically from those which were given by certain of the whites, but whatever the true cause may have been, young Pershing had nothing to do with that. He was simply obeying orders and doing his best in the war with the redmen who already confronted him.

Sitting Bull in particular was a strong and successful fighter. Crazy Horse, a bold and able chief, had, as the Sioux believed, been treacherously seized and bayoneted by the whites. Indeed, one of their rallying cries in the campaign was, "Remember our Chief, Crazy Horse."

General George A. Custer and nearly every one of his soldiers had been killed in a battle on the plains, in which the Indian leaders had succeeded in first surrounding Custer's force. Pa-he-hors-kah-zee (Long Yellow Hair), as the redmen had named Custer, was respected and greatly feared by them and for that reason they did their utmost to shoot him first of all when he finally took his stand in the center of the hollow square, into which he formed his troops when he discovered, after the breaking out of the battle, that he and his men were nearly surrounded.

The death of General Custer greatly angered

the whites, and it was promptly decided that once for all they would put an end to the uprisings of the strong and wily Sioux. This result, of course, was at last accomplished and in the final battle Lieutenant Pershing had his part. This battle, which the whites call Wounded Knee and the Indians term The Massacre at Wounded Knee Creek, was won when the troops finally surrounded the tepees of the redmen and then demanded that every gun should be given over.

This demand the Sioux refused, declaring that their experiences with the whites did not warrant them in making themselves entirely defenseless. They also explained that they themselves had bought and paid for every gun in the possession of the tribe.

This explanation or refusal was declared to be unsatisfactory. The command to attack quickly was given, the soldiers fired obediently and the report was made that they shot down every man, woman and child, with few exceptions, in the Indian village.

Thus the great Indian wars came to an end

and whatever may have been his feelings concerning the justice of the methods employed to subdue the Sioux, Lieutenant Pershing did not speak. He was a young officer and his part was not to explain, but to obey.

In September, 1891, he became Professor of Military Science and Tactics at the University of Nebraska.

CHAPTER V

A Military Instructor

At the University of Nebraska the young instructor-lieutenant revolutionized his department. It is said that when first the students presented themselves before him, according to the rules of the University, for drill, their preparations were nil and their appearance was far from being prepossessing. Previously the military drill had been more or less looked upon by the student body as a somewhat necessary but negligible and irksome task. Few prepared carefully for it and all were glad when the hour ended.

Under the new instructor the change was startling and immediate—and the college boys liked it. Among the strict demands of the new instructor was one that required every student when he appeared for drill to have his boots well blacked. Not only must the toes of the boots appear well, but every boy must see to it that the heels also received proper attention. Perhaps Lieutenant Pershing was interpreting for the Nebraska boys the familiar old proverb, "Black the heels of your boots."

The new professor speedily became popular, for no man is more unpopular in a student body than the teacher who weakly condones their neglect or too readily excuses their deficiencies. In spite of their protests to the contrary, they like the strict work and the fair and exacting teacher. And Pershing was liked—and liked more because he did not try to secure the good-will of his students.

The impression which the new instructor in military tactics made upon the student body is well shown by the following statement of the director of athletics in the University at that time, who naturally coöperated with the official representative of the Government whose influence over the college boys speedily became pronounced.

"He was the finest man I ever worked with," said Best. "It is true he was mighty strict with his work. but the results he got were so good that everybody he worked with loved him for it. When he was here we had a regiment the University could be proud of. I just worshipped that man and everybody around the University felt the same about him.

"Usually he was mighty dignified in his work, but he had a way of getting next to the new men.

"The boys at the University got a surprise the first time Pershing drilled them. It had been their habit before this time to come to drill with shoes blackened or not, just as they pleased. When Pershing took hold the first thing he looked at was to see that all shoes were well blackened and that the heels looked as good as the toes. He was just that thorough-going in everything all the time."—From the *New York Times*.

An incident recently told by one of his students in the University of Nebraska also is illustrative of the grip the drillmaster had upon the student body.

When Lieutenant Pershing later was appointed to a new position in the Army there was keen disappointment among the students, all of whom were his strong admirers. Certain of his cadets, who had profited greatly under his discipline and served under his orders, got together and decided that they wanted to wear badges of some kind. Gold medals were suggested, but for obvious reasons were not selected. Then one of the cadets suggested a plan as novel as it was new, and after a hearty laugh a delegation went to Lieutenant Pershing to ask for the gift of his riding trousers.

"Good Lord!" exclaimed the astonished instructor in tactics. "What do you want of my trousers?"

The students then explained their plan. They were to cut the trousers into such small bits that both the blue of the cloth and the yellow of the border would be found in every piece. Of these little strips they would make badges—one for every cadet.

The lieutenant promptly presented his visitors with his best pair.

One of the little band in relating the incident not long ago said, "We made the badges, which as far as I know were the first service badges ever used in the United States. If I could only buy, borrow, beg or steal one of those badges I'd readily wear it in France by the side of my ribbon of the Spanish-American war.''

With duties that were not arduous Lieutenant Pershing now not only continued his studies, particularly in strategy, but also found time to carry out the desire and plan that more or less had been in his thoughts since his boyhood—he took the course in law as it was given in the University. From this course he graduated and consequently was entitled to write another title after his name—that of Bachelor of Laws. He then was ''Professor'' Lieutenant John Joseph Pershing, A.B., ''Esquire.''

However, he was soon to become first lieutenant in the 10th U. S. Cavalry—a promotion which he received October 20, 1892. Joining his troop on October 11, 1895, he was again sent into the service with the 10th Cavalry at Fort Assinniboine, Montana, where he remained until October 16, 1896. In June and July of that year the monotony of life in the fort was varied by service in the field, where he assisted in deporting the Cree Indians.

A brief leave of absence followed this work on the frontier, but on December 17, 1896, he was assigned to duties at the Headquarters of the Army at Washington. This inside work, however, did not strongly appeal to the active young lieutenant, and in May of the following year he rejoined his regiment at Fort Assinniboine, Montana.

Here, however, his stay was to be very brief at this time. Promotion apparently had been slow, and doubtless many a time the heart of the ambitious young officer must have been somewhat heavy. The teachings of his father, however, were now bearing fruit and not for a moment did Lieutenant Pershing relax his steady, persistent labors. Whether recognition and promotion came or not he was to be prepared.

But the quiet, efficient young officer had not been unnoticed or forgotten by those who were higher in authority. At this time a new instructor in military tactics was needed in the United States Military Academy at West Point. What could be more natural than that the choice should fall upon Pershing? He was a hard worker, he had seen active service on the plains, he had learned· how to deal with men, and, besides, he had had actual experience in teaching tactics when he had been stationed at the University of Nebraska. And behind the experience was a personality quiet, modest and marvelously efficient. Lieutenant John Joseph Pershing was assigned to duty at the United States Military Academy as Assistant Instructor of Tactics, June 15, 1897.

To be back again in the well-remembered and beloved institution where he himself had been trained was a joy and honor. His devotion to and appreciation of West Point strengthened and intensified by his experiences in the years that had intervened since his graduation, we may be sure that the heart of Lieutenant Pershing was proud of the confidence which had been manifested in his selection to fill the vacant position.

Here again there was a continuance of his previous record of quiet and efficient service. It is true he was older now and he was more ready for the public and social duties of his position than perhaps he had been in his earlier days. And to the social side of his new task he responded as became one in his position.

It was not long, however, before a fresh opportunity presented itself—the one for which he had been waiting. The troubles between Spain and the Island of Cuba had for a considerable time been threatening to involve the United States. Many people sympathized with the Cubans in their longing and their efforts to secure their independence. The sturdy fight which the Islanders were making appealed strongly to many patriotic Americans who were glorying in the traditions of the struggle their own forefathers had made a century and a quarter earlier.

The friction between the United States and Spain steadily increased. The latter nation, perhaps not without a certain justification, was claiming that her colonists were fitting out expeditions and obtaining munitions and supplies for their soldiers in the cities of the United States, a supposedly neutral nation. She was not unnaturally irritated, too, by the steadily increasing numbers of Americans that were serving in the hard pressed and poorly equipped troops of Cuba. The culmination, however, came when the United States battleship, *Maine,* was blown up in the harbor of Havana, February 15, 1898. The long delayed declaration of war by the United States, April 21, 1898, was the speedy outcome.

CHAPTER VI

IN THE SPANISH WAR

LIEUTENANT PERSHING instantly grasped his long awaited opportunity. He resigned his position at West Point, and at once was sent to his regiment, the 10th Cavalry, then at Chicamauga, and afterwards near Tampa, Florida, but in June of that same year he went to Cuba and shared in the campaign against Santiago. Many have thought that the nickname "Black Jack" was affectionately given him because he was such a daring and dashing leader of the exceptionally brave black men of whom the 10th U. S. Cavalry at that time was composed.

In this campaign no official records can have quite the same human touch as the words of the modest young officer himself. In a lecture or address in the Hyde Park M. E. Church,

Chicago, November 27, 1898, the church whose founding was largely due to the interest and labors of his father,—Lieutenant Pershing described the experiences and deeds of his troop. The interest at the time was keen in the campaign he described. To-day, however, the interest is still keener in the young lieutenant who gave his vivid description of the battles in which he shared.

Address by Lieutenant Pershing at the Hyde Park M. E. Church, Chicago, at a patriotic Thanksgiving service, November 27, 1898:

The admonition of George Washington, "In peace prepare for war," had gone unheeded for one-third of a century. Congress had turned a deaf ear to the importunities of our military commanders. The staff departments of the army were only large enough to meet the ordinary necessities in times of peace of an army of 25,000 men. They had not transported even by rail for over thirty years a larger command than a regiment. In the face of all this every official both civil and military of staff and line seemingly did his best to overcome these adverse conditions and though of course mistakes were made I should hesitate to attribute to any individual other

66

than the purest motives of patriotism. The wonder is it was done at all. The wonder is it was done so well. The point of embarkation for the first army of invasion was Port Tampa, Florida. There was some delay in the embarkation due to various causes one of which was the inexperience of officers in transporting troops by water. Another cause of delay was uncertainty as to whether or not the Spanish fleet was really confined in the harbor of Santiago.

On the afternoon of June 14th, the fleet steamed out under its naval escort and a grander and more impressive sight the world has never seen.

Arriving in the vicinity of Santiago some time was spent in deciding where to attempt a landing. Two plans were proposed, one an attack from the west, which was said would involve, with the assistance of the navy, the capture of the outer defenses of the harbor of Sanitago. The other plan, the one which was adopted, ignored the existence of Morro Castle and the coast defenses and contemplated an attack on the city from the rear. This decided, a point of debarkation was selected at Daiquiri. There were no good maps of Cuba and very little was known of the coast or country.

At Daiquiri the navy prepared the way for landing by bombarding the town and driving out the Spanish troops who before leaving set fire to the buildings of the town and the machine shops and the mines located there. There were no docks at Daiquiri except a small wooden affair, old and out of repair.

The vessels could not go nearer than about 300 yards from the shore and then only in calm weather.

Nothing was taken ashore with the troops except what they carried on their backs, but the load was so heavy that to fall overboard in deep water meant to be drowned, though from the entire army but two men were lost.

On the morning of June 23d, the Tenth Cavalry, together with the First Cavalry and Roosevelt's Rough Riders and regiments which formed the second brigade of the cavalry division, were sent ashore and moved out northwest passing through Siboney to a point beyond the most advanced outposts toward Santiago. These troops though belonging to the cavalry were dismounted and in marching through marsh and bog overhung with boughs and vines, clad as they were in heavy clothing, they soon began to feel the wilting effects of the tropical sun; but every man had resolved for the honor of his country to make the best of the situation as a soldier and whether working or marching or fighting all behaved as though the success of the campaign depended upon their own individual efforts.

On July 10th, the day set for the ultimatum of the bombardment, the white flags of truce were again taken down and the men again climbed into the trenches. At four o'clock in the afternoon at the signal of the first gun from our northern battery the firing began and the battle raged with the same old fury as of those early July days; shells and bullets whistled violently for a few minutes but the enemy's fire gradually died away into silence. They realized their helplessness and the battle was over.

Our reinforcements had begun to arrive and the terms of capitulation dictated by the commanding general were soon agreed upon. On the morning of July 17th the lines of both armies were drawn up to witness the formal surrender. General Toral with an infantry escort rode out from the city to meet General Shafter, who was escorted by a squadron of mounted cavalry. The formalities were courteous though simple. Arms were presented by both commanders and the Spanish General tendered his sword to our commander.

General Shafter, accompanied by all the general and staff officers, his escort of cavalry and one regiment of infantry, then entered the city.

Shortly before twelve o'clock our troops were again drawn up in line along the six miles of trenches and stood at present arms. An officer ascended to the top of the Governor's palace and lowered the Spanish colors and now held the Stars and Stripes, impatient to declare our victory to the world. Suddenly at exactly twelve o'clock the enthusiasm burst forth, cannon boomed the national salute, bands played the Star Spangled Banner, hats were thrown into the air and ten thousand men as if to burst their throats joined in one grand American yell. There just beyond the hill outlined against the clear sky, over the Governor's palace in the captured city, though invisible to many of us, floated our own beloved flag. The campaign was over. For us the war was ended.

On June 29th a part of General Garcia's Army with some 4000 Cubans were marched to the front, but they rendered little assistance, either in working or fighting. The most of them fled at the first explosion of a Spanish shell over El Pozo Capital Hill on July 1st. However, some excuse is theirs. Ragged, some half naked, wearied from hunger, laden with huge earthen water pots, heavy packs and cooking utensils slung over their backs, armed with every conceivable obsolete pattern of gun, it is no wonder that they dared not face the deadly Mauser rifle; we ourselves had much less contempt for Spanish arms after we had met them face to face on the battle field.

On June 30th the general order came to move forward and every man felt that the final test of skill at arms would soon come. The cavalry division of six regiments camped in its tracks at midnight on El Pozo Hill, awoke next morning to find itself in support of Grimes' Battery which was to open fire here on the left.

The morning of July 1st was ideally beautiful; the sky was cloudless and the air soft and balmy; peace seem to reign supreme, great palms towered here and there above the low jungle. It was a picture of a peaceful valley. There was a feeling that we had secretly invaded the Holy Land. The hush seemed to pervade all nature as though she held her bated breath in anticipation of the carnage.

70

Captain Capron's field guns had opened fire upon the southern field at El Caney and the hill resounded with echoes. Then followed the reply of the musketry of the attacking invaders. The fighting in our front burst forth and the battle was on.

The artillery duel began and in company with foreign military attachés and correspondents we all sat watching the effect of the shots as men witness any fine athletic contest eagerly trying to locate their smokeless batteries. A force of insurgents near the old Sugar Mill cowered at the explosion of each firing charge apparently caring for little except the noise.

A slug of iron now and then fell among the surrounding bushes or buried itself deep in the ground near us. Finally a projectile from an unseen Spanish gun discharged a Hotchkiss piece, wounded two cavalrymen and smashed into the old Sugar Mill in our rear, whereupon the terrorized insurgents fled and were not seen again near the firing line until the battle was over.

When the Tenth Cavalry arrived at the crossing of San Juan River the balloon had become lodged in the treetops above and the enemy had just begun to make a target of it. A converging fire upon all the works within range opened upon us that was terrible in its effect. Our mounted officers dismounted and the men stripped off at the roadside everything possible and prepared for business.

We were posted for a time in the bed of the stream to the right directly under the balloon and stood in the water to our waists waiting orders to deploy. Remaining there under this galling fire of exploding shrapnel and deadly Mauser bullets the minutes seemed like hours. General Wheeler and a part of his staff stood mounted a few minutes in the middle of the stream. Just as I raised my hat to salute in passing up the stream to pass the squadron of my regiment, a piece of bursting shell struck between us and covered us both with water. Pursuant to orders from its commander, with myself as guide, the second squadron of the Tenth forced its way through wire fence and almost inpenetrable thicket to its position. The regiment was soon deployed as skirmishers in an opening across the river to the right of the road and our line of skirmishers being partly visible from the enemy's position, their fire was turned upon us and we had to lie down in the grass a few minutes for safety. Two officers of the regiment were wounded; here and there were frequent calls for the surgeon.

White regiments, black regiments, regulars and rough riders representing the young manhood of the North and South fought shoulder to shoulder unmindful of race or color, unmindful of whether commanded by an ex-confederate or not, and mindful only of their common duty as Americans.

Through streams, tall grass, tropical undergrowth, under barbed wire fences and over wire entanglements, regardless of casualties up the hill to the right this gallant advance was made. As we appeared on the brow of the hill we found the Spaniards retreating only to take up a new position farther on, spitefully firing as they retreated and only yielding their ground inch by inch.

Our troopers halted and laid down but momentarily to get a breath and in the face of continued volleys soon formed for attack on the block houses and intrenchments on the second hill. This attack was supported by troops including some of the Tenth who had originally moved to the left toward this second hill and had worked their way in groups slipping through the tall grass and bushes, crawling when casualties came too often, courageously facing a sleet of bullets and now hung against the steep southern declivity ready to spring the few remaining yards into the teeth of the enemy. The fire from the Spanish position had doubled in intensity. There was a moment's lull and our line moved forward to the charge across the valley separating the two hills. Once begun it continued dauntless in its steady, dogged, persistent advance until like a mighty resistless challenge it dashed triumphant over the crest of the hill and firing a parting volley at the vanishing foe planted the silken standard on the enemy's breastworks and the Stars and Stripes over the block house on San Juan Hill to stay.

This was a time for rejoicing. It was glorious.

* * * * *

But among the scenes of rejoicing there was others of sadness. Both American and Spanish troops lay dead and wounded around us; all were cared for alike. I saw a colored trooper stop at a trench filled with Spanish dead and wounded and gently raise the head of a wounded Spanish lieutenant and give him the last drop of water from his own canteen. Their dead, of whom there were many, had fought bravely and we buried them in the trenches where they gallantly fell.

The losses of the day were heavy—the Tenth Cavalry losing one-half of its officers and twenty per cent of its men. We officers of the Tenth Cavalry have taken our black heroes in our arms. They had again fought their way into our affections, as they here had fought their way into the hearts of the American people. Though we had won, it had cost us dearly.

An attempt was made that evening to recapture the hill, but our defense was so strong that the attempt was futile; the Spaniards retreating to their first interior line of intrenchments 300 to 500 yards away.

The firing on both sides was kept up until dark and ceased only at intervals during the night. Over El Caney the battle had raged all day, but steadily as the Spaniards had held their positions the fierce charges of the gallant Seventh, Twelfth and Twenty-fifth regiments of infantry were resistless. Soon after San Juan was ours, El Caney fell.

By morning the position was strengthened so that our line was fairly well protected, reveillé was sounded by Spanish small arms and artillery in chorus, but the signal had been anticipated and all men were in their places at the firing line.

Daylight was breaking in the east when both sides began where they had left off the night before and the firing all day was incessant. A few moments after the firing opened, some cannoneers permitted a limber from one of the guns of the light battery near us to get away and it went rolling down the hillside to the rear for a quarter of a mile. Our artillery was silenced by the enemy's small arms and compelled to take up a new position; strong shrapnel went screeching over head and bursting beyond. The adjutant of my regiment was stricken by a hidden sharpshooter. The heat soon became intense and there was no shelter and cannon balls plunged through the lines at the top of the hill and went rolling to the bottom of the valley; bullets spattered against the isolated trees or grazed the newly made earthworks covering with dirt the men in the trenches and fairly mowing the grass for many yards in our front. Thus the day went on and the night and the succeeding day began. Then came the welcome truth; everybody drew a long breath and thanked God; it was possible once more to walk erect; however, the echoes of the last three days were slow to die away and at the breaking of a bough or the rusting of a leaf there was a temptation to duck.

At noon on July 4th the regiments were formed into line and I had the pleasure of reading to my regiment a telegram from the President extending the thanks and congratulations of the American people to the army in front of Santiago for its gallantry and success.

The brave Linares, however, had already realized the hopelessness of his cause, but he would not surrender without permission from his home government. Therefore the city must be bombarded. Pacificos and the non-combatants were ordered out of the city and were permitted to come within our lines. All day long on the dusty road leading from Santiago to El Caney passed the long white line; faint, hungry women carried a bundle of clothing and parcel of food or an infant while helpless children trailed wearily at the skirts of their wretched mothers. An old man tottered along on his cane and behind him a puny lad and an aged woman; old and young women and children and decrepit men of every class—those refined and used to luxury together with the ragged beggar—crowding each other in this narrow column. It was a pitiful sight; from daylight to dark the miserable procession trooped past. The suffering of the innocent is not the least of the sorrows of war.

The days of truce and hostilities alternated; all roll calls were suspended except the sunset call and retreat on days of truce.

At the evening call we daily ceased our chatting, cooking or working and groups or lines of officers and men stood with uncovered heads in respectful and reverent attention as the music of the Star Spangled Banner and the sight of the flag we had planted on the hill above us, lifted us out of ourselves and carried us in thought to home and country; it was the soldiers' silent Ave Maria.

Duty in the trenches was no less arduous because of the few days of truce; all the available men would report to work at strengthening positions and building bomb-proof shelters. Vigilance never relaxed until the capitulation. The rainy season had set in in earnest and the trenches were at times knee deep with mud and water. The constant exposures to the heat and rain together with the strain of battle began to have its effect upon even the strongest of us. Our sick list gradually grew and the dreaded yellow fever appeared in our ranks; the field hospitals already overcrowded with wounded were compelled to accommodate the increasing number of fever patients; medical supplies and food for the sick were lacking and though many things were furnished by the Red Cross there was yet a shortage.

Since July 3d the firing from the Spanish trenches had become irregular, desultory and non-effective. Our artillery gunners now knew the range of every Spanish battery and our men in the trenches—every one a trained marksman—knew the distance of every Spanish position. A Spanish captain told me afterward that it was dangerous for them even to stick up a finger for fear of having it shot off; and yet the Spanish commander still held out.

The literary style of the young lecturer reveals the direct virile qualities that since have made General Pershing one of the most forceful and clear American writers on topics having to do with the military affairs of the country. His use of adjectives perhaps is somewhat freer than in his later writings, but there is the same vivid, direct power of expression and description. His modesty at the time prevented him from referring to the fact that twice he was recommended for brevet commissions in the war with Spain for "personal gallantry and untiring energy and faithfulness." Nor did he mention the words of General Baldwin, a brave soldier of the Civil War, who said of him: "Pershing is the coolest man under fire I ever saw." And he makes no mention of the earnest protest of a certain foreign officer, the representative of his own government in the Santiago campaign, who begged the daring troops not to make the now famous charge up San Juan Hill because they would be rushing into certain death.

The official records, however, are now available and consequently we are not dependent upon stories which occasionally seem to possess a snow-ball like quality of increasing in size as they gain in distance from their starting points.

Headquarters, Tenth U. S. Cavalry,
  Camp Hamilton, Cuba, July, 1898.
Adjutant General, Second Brigade, Cavalry Division,
    Fifth Army Corps.
  Sir:—I have the honor to submit the following report of the part taken by the Tenth Cavalry in the battle of July 12th and 13th, 1898, before Santiago de Cuba.

On the morning of July 1st the regiment, consisting of troops, A, B, C, D, E, F, G, I, field and staff, occupying a position on the left of the second cavalry, directed the line extending nearly north and south on a ridge some three or four miles from Santiago.

At about 6:30 A. M. a battery of artillery massed a short distance from our right opened upon the works of Santiago, the regiment being exposed to much of the return fire of the American batteries. After the artillery fire had ceased the regiment moved right past the sugar mills and proceeded in rear of the town on the road toward Santiago. The movement was delayed as we approached the San Juan river and the regiment came within range of fire about half a mile from the crossing. Upon reaching the river I found that the Seventy-first N. Y. Volunteers were at the crossing and that the regiment preceding mine had moved to the right. The Tenth Cavalry was here subject to and confronting radically an infantry fire from the three block houses and intrenchments in front and the works farther to the left and nearer Santiago. The fire was probably drawn by a balloon which preceded the regiment to a point near the ford where it was held. I was directed to take a position to the right behind the river, however, for potection moving to this position and while there the regiment suffered considerable loss. After an interval of 20 to 30 minutes I was directed to form line of battle in a particularly open field facing toward the blockhouse and strong intrenchments to the north occupied by the enemy. Much difficulty was found on account of the dense undergrowth crossed in several directions by wire fences. As a part of the cavalry division under General Sumner, the regiment was formed on two lines. The first squadron under Major S. T. Norvall consisting of troops A, E, B and I leading. The second line under Major T. J. Wint consisting of troops C, F and G. Troop D having crossed further down the river attached itself to a command of infantry and moved with that command on the two blockhouses. The regiment advanced in this formation under a heavy fire from the enemy's position proceeding but a short distance when the two lines were reunited into one. The advance was rapidly continued in an irregular line toward the blockhouses and intrenchments to the right front. During this advance the lines passed some troops of the first cavalry which I think had been previously formed on our right. Several losses occurred before reaching the top of them; first lieutenant W. H. Smith being killed as he arrived at its crest. The enemy having retreated toward the northwest toward the second and third blockhouses, new lines were formed and rapid advance was made upon the new positions.

The regiment assisted in capturing these works from the enemy and with the exception of Troops C and I who had joined the first volunteer cavalry, then took up a position north of the second blockhouse, remaining there during the night. With some changes in the positions of troops they held this line of the second and third under a heavy and continuous fire from the enemy's intrenchments in front and the regiment now occupying a part of the advance intrenched positions. Some troops lost their relative positions in line during the first day of the battle but attached themselves to others and continued to move forward. During the entire engagement the regiment acted with exceptional coolness and bravery. It held its position at the ford and moved forward unflinchingly after deploying through the advance under the heavy fire from the enemy's works.

The officers and men in general throughout exhibited great bravery obeying orders with unflinching alacrity while attacking with small arms an enemy strongly posted in intrenchment and block-house supported with artillery. Words cannot express my gratification at such conduct and I would request such service receive some special recognition. It is difficult to distinguish between officers and men all of whom are so deserving but of the officers whose conduct on the field came under my direct personal observation I would especially mention Major S. T. Norvall, Major T. J. Wint, squadron commander, first lieutenant J. J. Pershing, quartermaster, and first lieutenant M. H. Bowman, adjutant, for their untiring energy, faithfulness and gallantry during this engagement and would recommend the officers mentioned for brevet commissions, . . .

Very respectfully,
(s) T. A. BALDWIN,
Lieutenant Colonel, Tenth Cavalry,
Commanding.

[A TRUE COPY]
Second lieutenant, Tenth Cavalry, acting regimental adjutant.

"A foreign officer standing near our position when we started to make that charge was heard to say, 'Men, for Heaven's sake don't go up that hill. It is impossible for human beings to take that position and you cannot stand the fire.' Notwithstanding this with a terrific yell we rushed up to the enemy's works and you know the result. Men who were near said that when this officer saw us make the charge he turned his back and wept."

Camp A. G. Forse,
Huntsville, Ala., December 1, 1898.

The Adjutant General, U. S. Army,
  Washington, D. C.,

Through military channels,

Sir: I have the honor to submit the following report of the part taken by Troop D, Tenth Cavalry, in the engagement before Santiago de Cuba so far as it is known to me. As we approached the foot of the hill our artillerymen fired over our heads at the enemy on top of it. This caused a slowing up on the general advance. When I was about half way up the hill I was disabled by three bullet wounds received simultaneously. I had already received one, but did not know it. What took place after my disablement is known to me only through the statement of my men and others subsidized by the depositions enclosed herewith. My platoon went to the top of the hill with the infantry and was soon afterward conducted by Lieutenant J. J. Pershing, R. O. M., Tenth Cavalry, to the line of the Tenth Cavalry some distance to the right.

Very respectfully,
John Bigelow, Jr.,
Tenth Cavalry, Commanding,
Troop D.

In the report of Major Wint, November 28th, 1898, to the adjutant-general is the following: "Lieutenant Pershing, R.O.M., was with the Second Squadron when passed on Sugar House Hill and during its advance on San Juan Hill he conducted himself in a most gallant and efficient manner."

The war with Spain was soon terminated but the executive ability of Lieutenant Pershing was still in demand. The period of reconstruction was difficult then, as it always is, presenting problems different from those of active fighting, but no less puzzling and perplexing. In this trying time we find him serving as an executive under the direction of the War Department and manifesting in his quiet, persistent way the same qualities of efficiency which had marked his career up to this time. On August 18, 1898, he was serving as Major Chief Ordnance Officer with the United States Volunteers, remaining on duty at the Headquarters of the Army until December 20, 1898, and then on duty in the office of the Assistant Secretary of War, under whom he organized the Bureau of Insular Affairs, and was at the head of that Bureau until the following August. On May 12, 1899, he was honorably discharged from Volunteer service and on June 6, 1899, he was Major and Assistant Adjutant General, United States Volunteers.

Office and work of detail did not, however, appeal strongly to him. Having known the life and work in the field, and also possessed of a temperament that demanded more active work and out-of-door life that an office provided, at his own request he was sent to the Philippine Islands and was assigned to duty as Adjutant General of the District of Mindanao and Jolo (afterwards a Department under the same name).

He became captain in the First Cavalry, February, 1901, and on August 20th of the same year he was transferred to the Fifteenth Cavalry. His work in the Philippine Islands continued and there his soldierly qualities found a larger field for development and activity than they had known before.

85

CHAPTER VII

IN THE PHILIPPINES

THE supreme testing of Pershing up to this time in his career came in the Philippines. There he was dealing with a strange people who for three centuries had learned their lessons and formed their opinions of the white men from their contact and dealings with the Spaniards, of whom they had seen chiefly the adventurers or those who for the "good of their country" had fled from their homes. To such men the exploitation of the "natives" was a legitimate game and the little brown men had thoroughly learned to play their part in it.

The provinces in which Pershing was to find his field of activity were as difficult as any in the islands. For years the natives had been accustomed to import arms from Borneo and elsewhere. Certain of the tribes were famous also for their skill as forgers of swords, krises and barongs. Every datto had numbers of lantaka or brass cannon and was well skilled in the use of them. Pershing's problem was not only to subdue these men,—farmers, artificers and all alike fighters after their own manner, but he must also at the same time convince them of the good will and helpful intentions of the new Government, which for a time and for their own good was now to control them. Naturally suspicious, treacherous in many ways, the Islands presented difficulties that well might have staggered the young officer.

General Pershing's first term of service in the Philippines was from 1899 to 1903. In the interval between his first and second terms of service as soldier and governor in the Islands, he was back in the United States to serve on the General Staff and also was serving as military attaché in the army of General Kuroki in the war between Russia and Japan.

In his first years in the Philippines his work was of a character that made him known to the Army and to the authorities at Washington, but it did not make him widely known to his countrymen.

Briefly stated, his record during his two terms of service in the Philippines is as follows: he was in the field November, 1900, to March, 1901, against General Capistrano, the commander of the insurrectionary forces; he was in command of an expedition against the hostile Moros of Maciu, starting from Camp Vicars, Mindanao, September 18, 1902. In the actions at Guam, September 18, and at Bayabao, September 20, 1902, he had a responsible part. On September 29, 1902, he captured Fort Moru, driving the Moros from that Peninsula on that date. He attacked the Moros at Maciu, September 30, 1902, capturing their two forts and then returned to Camp Vicars October 3, 1902. He was again in action at Bacolod, April 6-8, 1903, and again at Calabui April 9, 1903, and Iaraca River, May 4, 1903. He commanded the first military force that ever encircled Lake Lanao.

In May, 1902, General Chaffee was desirous

of securing a young leader to deal with the troublesome and specific problem in the province of Zamboanga, where the fierce and turbulent little Moros dwelt. Many of these people were Mohammedans and had been taught that the swiftest and surest way to secure happiness in the next world was by the slaughter of Christians in this present world. During 300 years they had fought the Spanish invaders, whose every attempt to subdue them had failed.

Pershing in command of five troops of the Fifteenth Cavalry, together with a battery of artillery, a company of engineers and a battalion of the Twenty-seventh Infantry, was stationed at Camp Vicars in the Lake Lanao District of Mindanao. He had taken the place made vacant by the promotion of Colonel Baldwin.

Although the Americans had obtained a foothold on the southern side of Lake Lanao, very few of them had actually become friendly. In fact the Spaniards, in all the years of their occupation, had never subdued the main tribes to subordination.

Among those who especially defied the American authority was the Sultan of Bacalan and 600 of his followers who occupied a stronghold on the western side of Lake Lanao from which they made almost daily forays. Walls of earth and bamboo some 20 feet in thickness had been added to the natural defenses of the position they selected. A moat 40 feet wide and 30 feet deep surrounded the position. The defenders thought it was proof against any possible attack. Friendly overtures failed to make an impression upon their leaders, and their cotta was finally surrounded and their surrender demanded. Still confident of their prowess, they declined to accede to the American Commander's demands and the latter was compelled to assault this strong fortification. Accordingly trees were felled and used to make a crossing over the moat and when all was in readiness the place was taken in a fierce hand-to-hand encounter between the Americans and the Moros. The American success was complete and a severe lesson was taught to Moros in that region. General Pershing completed the conquest of Mindanao Moros by marching his command entirely around Lake Lanao through the dense jungles and swamps bordering the lake.

As a matter of interest several reports made by General Pershing on his work in the Philippines follow, and some in which reference is made to him by certain of his superior officers at that time.

In the later reports sent by Pershing there is manifest the same painstaking carefulness and thorough understanding of his task. He makes recommendations concerning the distribution of the troops in the Philippines, goes into detail about the necessity and the location of cold storage plants, and has positive convictions as to what changes ought to be made in the Subsistence Department. Certain posts also ought to be made permanent. He clearly presents the reasons leading to his conclusions.

Annual Report of the Lieutenant General commanding the Army—1901

The command left Cagayan, December 16th, under Major Case, accompanied by Major J. J. Pershing, adjutant general, department of Mindanao and Jolo.

factual incident

In a narrow gorge 800 feet deep formed by the river the insurgents were found in three strongly constructed forts which our troops attacked without loss. The enemy must have suffered severely, but his loss was not ascertained. Two cannon fell into our hands. The 18th and 19th of December were consumed in surrounding the stronghold of Maxajambos by gaining a position commanding Langaran to the south of Maxajambos. Langaran, which was the headquarters of the insurgents, was entered on the 20th and considerable quantity of provisions, ammunitions of war, cuartels, etc., were found and destroyed. The insurrectos had made good their escape under cover of darkness.

On the 28th, the insurgents were discovered a mile and a half south of Langaran occupying a strong position which our troops succeeded in reaching and the enemy was forced to retreat in disorder. The command then moved on to Talacao but was not met by any resistance. Such buildings as had been used by the insurgents for storehouses, etc., were destroyed as well as supplies. One prisoner was taken. The surrounding country was thoroughly scouted without encountering any enemy force. The troops returned to Cagayan the 31st of December.

From the report of Captain James J. Mays, 40th Infantry, concerning the attack on Cagayan, December 16th to 25th, 1900:

He reports, "late in the afternoon of December 17th insurgents concealed in the brush fired on horses that were being watered in the cañon. Major Pershing, who was with the command, took fifteen men on one bluff and I took about the same number on another and poured volleys into the cañon, firing at smoke from insurgent pieces, silencing their fire. I think we killed some of them, but do not know. The following morning Major Pershing crossed the river and joined Captain Millar. Captain Millar threw shells into Maxajambos and signaled that the place seemed deserted. During the day I kept patrols on the plateau. Señor Cruz came out on the morning of this day and I sent him to Captain Millar. I questioned him about the plan of cutting through the timber. He said he never heard of anyone getting through there and that it would be very difficult on account of the cañon, and also that it would end on top of a cliff 400 or 500 feet high. I concluded not to attempt it."

To the Headquarters Department of Mindanao and Jolo.

Cagayan de Misamis, P. I.

February 2, 1901.

The Commanding Officer, Provincial District of Mindanao and Jolo.

Sir: I am instructed by the department commander to advise you that General Capistrano, commanding the insurgent forces in Northern Mindanao, has signified his wish to meet the department commander in conference and to direct that you take whatever measures are possible to insure his safe conduct accompanied by his staff and that of any tribes with a pass signed by the commanding general and countersigned by the adjutant general. Patrols and expeditionary forces need not be suspended but should be warned to be at special pains not to molest unresisting parties of natives and to take special care not to interfere with individuals or squadrons, to indicate that their mission is peaceful.

Very respectfully,

J. J. PERSHING,
Assistant Adjutant General.

To the Headquarters Department of Mindanao and Jolo.

Cagayan de Misamis, P. I.

February 28, 1901.

To the Commanding Officer, 1st District of Mindanao and Jolo.

SIR: I am instructed by the Department commander to invite your attention to the fact that there are at this place ten prisoners of war either now or recently officers in the insurgent forces. With one or two exceptions these officers have voluntarily surrendered one at a time and have been induced to do so with a distinct understanding that they would not be closely confined or otherwise molested so long as they refrained from all conduct which might be construed as hostile to the United States.

It is understood that most of these have severed their connections with the insurgent forces and have thrown up their appointments as officers.

You will please assemble these men, give them strict, but fair limits of arrest, extending in no case beyond the limits of the town of Cagayan de Misamis and inform them that any violation of their obligations as prisoners of war, however slight, will be followed by immediate arrest and deportation from the Philippine Islands to Guam; also that they are to report daily in a body at a stated hour to the Provost Marshal.

The Department Commander further directs that you assemble all the more prominent citizens of this and adjoining towns who are known or suspected of being in sympathy with the insurgents and inform them that they must refrain absolutely from giving aid or comfort to them and without communicating with the insurgent forces in any manner under penalty of immediate arrest and deportation.

In carrying out the terms of this order you are directed to exercise considerable vigilance and the most drastic vigor.

Very respectfully,

J. J. PERSHING,
Assistant Adjutant General.

CHAPTER VIII

SUBJECTING THE MOROS

THE first period of General Pershing's service in the Philippine Islands lasted until 1903. He then was recalled to the United States and became a member of the General Staff Corps. This position he held until 1906.

Within that time, however, he was appointed the military attaché at Tokio, Japan, and was with General Kuroki in the latter's campaign in the war between Japan and Russia. It is said that his report forwarded to our Government is one of the most lucid and forceful military documents ever received by the Department.

If any discouragements had come to the young officer in his lonely campaigns in the jungles of the Philippines and he had felt that somehow he had been banished to a region where his services of necessity would never be recognized, that thought was banished by the action of President Roosevelt in 1906.

His services in the First and Fifteenth Cavalry as well as his activities in Washington and his report as the military attaché of his Government, had brought him very strongly before the attention of the President, who now was eager to reward him for his faithful services.

There were certain obstacles, however, in the way, and the President did his utmost to secure the proper legislation to enable him to reward the soldier whom he was eager to honor. There were delays, however, and the delays continued. Red tape exerted its binding force upon the makers of the laws and no apparent progress was made.

Thereupon President Roosevelt in his direct way determined to wait no longer for changes in the laws. Promptly he nominated Pershing to be Brigadier General; the nomination was confirmed and the long deferred recognition was now manifest.

He had labored in somewhat obscure fields.

He had assisted in subduing insurrections, had supervised many local improvements in the territory within which he was working. He had assisted in winning victories and had warded off attacks by hostile Moros. There had, however, been nothing spectacular in his work. His reliability, good sense, bravery and administrative ability, however, were now better known and he was in every way prepared for the more important problems which now confronted him.

The President by his action had raised or "jumped" the new general eight hundred and sixty-two orders. Worthy as the honor was and worthily bestowed, for a time there were protests from disappointed seekers after office. Some cried "politics," but as a rule these objections came in loudest tones from those who by devious ways had sought certain "pulls" for their own elevation. Personal ambitions and personal jealousies, perhaps, also entered to a degree and aided not a little in delaying the legislation which President Roosevelt desired.

Doubtless this condition deeply hurt General Pershing, but there was no complaining on his part. It was his to show that he was not unworthy of his new honor. Years before he had been taught by his father that to be worthy of promotion was more than the promotion itself. And now he was soon to return to the Philippines to show in the jungle and on the field, in council and administration, that the action of the President had not been the result of idle or thoughtless impulse.

Not long before this time, on January 26, 1905, General Pershing was married. There is a current story, for the truthfulness of which the writer cannot vouch, that when the nomination of Major Pershing for promotion was placed before the Senate, there was made at the same time a just and true statement of the distinguished services he had rendered his country in his career in the Philippines. In the visitors' gallery with friends, intently listening to the proceedings, was Miss Frances Warren, daughter of United States Senator Warren of Wyoming. As she listened to the words spoken concerning the American officer in the Philippines it is said she remarked, "What a wonderful record. I should like to see the man who made it." Not long afterward she did see him though the meeting was entirely unexpected. Doubtless the man impressed her more than had his praises to which she had listened in the halls of Congress, for on January 26, 1905, she became Mrs. John Joseph Pershing.

The general, who for years had been compelled to live a somewhat lonely life, whose activities had kept him far from friends and his own people, was now to have the help and comfort of the strong and beautiful daughter of Senator Warren. Never effusive nor one to refer to his personal or private affairs, his friends nevertheless have told of the deep love of the General for his wife and family—a tragic setting for the terrible tragedy which later in a moment disrupted his home and deprived him forever of his wife and three little daughters.

Directly after the wedding, he was ordered to Japan as Military Attaché and upon arrival

immediately joined the forces of General Kuroki in Manchuria, as has been said, as the representative of the Army of the United States
in the war between Japan and Russia. This
gave him an opportunity to witness the conduct
of modern war, which was afterwards to prove
of great value to him as a soldier.

In 1907 he returned to the Philippines for a
time, but it was not until 1909 that he returned
as Governor of the Moro Province. From that
time on his work in the Philippines was not
unlike that in which he formerly had been engaged.

The raids of the Moros on the coast towns
had been checked by the brilliant victory at
Bayan, but during the succeeding years the
Moros in general had continued very hostile.
Many tribes were very obdurate and their long
experience with the Spaniards made them confident of their own ability.

Early in his career as Governor of the Moro
Province General Pershing decided that the
only way to insure peace among the Moros was
to disarm them entirely, as up to that time they

had always been allowed to carry both firearms and their cutting weapons. When the edict as to disarming the Moros went forth, the hitherto hostile elements of the Sulu Islands went on the warpath. Although every means had been exhausted to induce the Moros to lay down their arms and become peaceful citizens their independent habits of centuries were not thus easily given up. The first clash came at Mt. Dajo, where several hundred Moros, who had refused to give up their arms, had assembled to defy the authorities. After all efforts at argument proved futile, General Pershing, with 500 American troops and an equal number of Philippine Scouts, suddenly surrounded Mt. Dajo. The movement of troops was difficult through the jungle, where, in many places, the troops were compelled to cut a pathway, in doing which they were exposed to sudden and fierce attacks by fanatical Moros.

Not a day was lost and Mt. Dajo was surrounded. Quietly the leader remarked that he would "take the place if it took ten years to capture it"—a remark that reminds one of a similar declaration by another American soldier that he would "fight it out on this line if it takes all summer."

First, his jungle fighters cut a trail entirely around the base of the mountain, at the same time doing their utmost to protect themselves against attacks from the Moros, who were as skillful in this work as they were in nearly every phase of fighting in the jungle. The men were compelled also to protect themselves from attacks from above, for it was a favorite method of the Moros by unexpected attacks, in rushes of wild fury, to scatter their enemies when they tried to ascend.

The soldiers speedily formed a complete cordon around the mountain and the siege promptly began. Pershing knew what the Moros did not know that he knew,—that when they had withdrawn to their stronghold they had done so in such haste that they neglected or were unable to bring with them supplies sufficient for a long siege. Not many days would pass before the necessity of obtaining food would compel them to try to break the iron ring about them and to send out parties for help.

Pershing's information soon proved to be correct. After a few days, in small detachments the Moros did their utmost to gain the open jungle by dashing through the surrounding lines. But every dash was frustrated, although the fanatical fighters recklessly threw themselves into what was certain death. The failure of one band to break through was merely a clarion call to others of their fellows to renew the attempt. The mad and useless efforts were all baffled.

At last on Christmas Day, 1911, the Moros in the little fortress did what Moros had not done before,—they marched down the mountain side and surrendered,—that is, all did save a few who made a final wild attempt to break through the jungle. The effort was vain, however, for the regulars hotly pursued the little brown fighters and the desperadoes paid the penalty of their daring.

Soon the brown fighters were convinced and promptly acted accordingly. They discovered that they were dealing with a leader different from any they had previously known. He did exactly what he said he would do. His promise could be trusted. His word was reliable; and forty forts soon were given over to the Americans.

This constituted a tremendous tribute to Pershing. The yellow man does not usually trust the white man on account of many unfortunate experiences he has had. But now all this was changed.

The subjection of all the Moros, however, had not yet been accomplished. Some still distrusted the white men and, as they believed, fought to retain and defend their homes. At last, however, at the Battle of Bagsag in June, 1913, the task was completed, though Pershing's work was not yet all done. What he had believed to be only a temporary task had now assumed larger and longer proportions. He had done so well that he was retained not only in command but also was the Governor of the newly conquered, but not yet friendly province. Perhaps there is no better proof of the ability and sterling character of General Pershing anywhere to be found than the fact that the little brown Moros whom he defeated and overthrew, later made him a datto of their tribe—an official position that granted him full power of life and death over every man, woman and child in their numbers and also made him a judge as well as a ruler over them.

In his quiet, efficient, modest manner General Pershing in a larger way had manifested the same qualities that had marked the lad at Laclede, the student at West Point, and the young lieutenant leading his black troops in Cuba. To-day all Americans are proud as well as pleased that there were leaders able to recognize, and brave enough to reward, the services of a soldier who had filled with honor every position to which he had been assigned.

In the reports to the War Department there are many interesting incidents descriptive of the daring and labors of General Pershing, who was not only in command of the troops, but also, as has been said, the military governor of the Province of Mindanao. In his own reports there are general as well as specific recommendations and the directness with which he states what to him appear to be needful for the good of the Filipinos as well as of the American troops, is marked.

[From the Report of June 30, 1910.]

To the Adjutant-General of the United States Army:

To keep down the lawless element among the Moros and pagan tribes a relatively large force must be maintained in this department. We have now occupied these Islands long enough to determine quite definitely where such posts should be located. There should be a regiment post on the Island of Jolo, a brigade post in the Lake Lanoa division and the regimental post in some point in the vicinity of Zamboanga, besides smaller posts at Fort Overton and Malabang.

Jolo is the strategical site for the post in the Sulu Archipelago. From there any point in the Island can be quickly reached and the other islands of the Sulu group can be easily controlled. It possesses a good harbor and is otherwise well situated as a military station. Mounted troops can go anywhere on the Island and they exert more influence over the Moros than dismounted troops.

The Lake Lanoa Moros are turbulent and unruly and the presence of a relatively large force in that region will be required for years to come. The shores of Lake Lanoa afford a very desirable place for a military post. The country is very fertile and in case of necessity troops could maintain themselves there almost indefinitely.

The erection of a permanent post at Zamboanga is in every way desirable. Troops located at Zamboanga could be sent to any place in the department more quickly than from any other point.

After stating that many of the barracks and quarters will not last long, he comments:

Permanent posts should be built entirely of concrete or of a combination of concrete and most durable hard woods.

The khaki uniform furnished by the quartermasters' department for tropical service is poorly made and ill-fitting. The American made cotton khaki cloth is heavy, shrinks badly, fades rapidly and is almost as warm as woolen cloth. This clothing is as poor an excuse for a military uniform as can be imagined. Instead of offering inducements to soldiers to enter and remain in foreign service by giving them good-looking and well-fitted clothes, we force upon them these unbecoming, hot, heavy, ill-fitting uniforms. The best khaki cloth is of English manufacture and should be prescribed for the army.

It is light, cool, holds its color and does not shrink. All uniform cloth ought to be manufactured by tailors enlisted for the purpose.

He goes on to discuss the water supply, public animals, ships and drydocks, and pack and wagon transportation, water and sewer systems, the roads and the works, ice and cold storage plants and also makes suggestions for the engineering and ordnance departments. He asks for the construction, for military purposes, of a telegraph line of communication with the District of Davao. He speaks also of the marked improvement in the target practice, especially in small arms. He gives the details of the eighteen expeditions entered upon and has a complete description of the Subano uprising, which occurred in November, 1909, among the hill people of Zamboanga. Certain Moro chiefs from Lake Lanoa, assisted by pagan and Christian outcasts and criminals from the Misamis Strip, planned to gather the hill people into an inaccessible part of the "Bolman Country." This plan was carried out by resorting to false prophecies, and, in many cases, to violence. Thousands of these small pastoral Subanos were driven into camps, where they would be more completely under the control of these self-appointed leaders. Large camps were built, one at Bolman and one at Dampalan, and preparations were made for defending them. The positions were well selected. The occupants were armed with spears, krises, kampilans and barongs. A constabulary force from Capitan was sent November 28th, by the Governor of the Moro provinces, to the outskirts of the Barbon camp. The Subanos, under the leadership of their Moro chiefs, attacked the constabulary with spears, and several of the men were killed. Upon the call of the Provincial Governor for troops, the second company of Philippine scouts, commanded by Captain Moses T. Barlow, was sent to Dipolog to report to Major John J. Finley, Governor of the District of Zamboanga, who was placed in command.

In the report of Major Finley that officer writes:

"The considerable reward offered for the apprehension of the leaders did not stimulate the natives to search for them. The Subanos were thoroughly subdued and terrorized by the rigorous discipline of the camp and after the fight of November 28th they were only too glad to hide themselves in the woods and mountains. The Philippines made no effort whatever to earn the reward.

"Ample time was given for the hill people to take a look at the troops and become convinced that this form of governmental power was friendly and really interested in their salvation and prosperity. After becoming thus convinced, the good influence of the government spread with rapidity among the Subanos. They returned to their farms by hundreds daily, they proferred their services to the government and declined remuneration. The important witnesses emerged from their hiding places and the apprehension of the leaders became a possibility. The leaders were caught, the witnesses came forward from their hiding places to convict them, and the wondering Subanos reclaimed their homes and began life anew. There was a general rejoicing among them."

He reports a shortage of officers and states that two-year troops hardly get acquainted with the people or really become interested in the larger problems that are being worked out under American control. "The army cannot do itself full justice in the administration of civil affairs in a Moro Province unless the period of service be extended." He declares that service in the Philippine Islands is not more arduous than service in Texas or Arizona. "There is no reason why enlisted men should be given credit for double service for every year spent in the Islands."

He reports also that the Philippine Scouts are in excellent condition. A high state of discipline exists among them. Their officers are enthusiastic and willing, and the same spirit extends to the men.

In 1911, similar reports are made concerning uniforms, clothing, etc. The general good health of the soldiers is described. Only three cases of typhoid fever occurred in the entire department. "Too much time is devoted to target practice in comparison with other classes of training. The increased pay for expert riflemen, sharpshooters and marksmen does not serve to increase appreciation and the efficiency in rifle fire." He recommended that extra pay be discontinued.

He reports nineteen expeditions of the troops and gives a clear account of the pagan uprising. He urges an increase in the regular regiments of infantry in time of peace, to form a substantial basis in the first line when war comes. "Under no circumstances should the enlisted strength of a regiment be less than one thousand men, in time of peace. In war this should be increased to two thousand four hundred or even three thousand." He recommends that the cavalry regiments be made smaller. He states that the efficiency of the cavalry is not as high as it should be, while the field artillery is below the recognized requirements. The Philippine Scouts sometimes are inclined to consider themselves on the same footing as the white troops, with a consequent disinclination to perform duties away from well-equipped and centrally located garrisons.

"Considering their low cost of maintenance I believe it poor policy not to keep them up to the authorized maximum strength of 12,000, reducing the garrison of American troops accordingly.

"I believe the time is propitious for the organization of Philippine cavalry, mounted on hardy native ponies which require none of the expensive hay of the American horse.

"The post exchange ought to be authorized to sell beer and light wines. Conducted under proper regulations and under official supervision this feature formerly served as a means to furnish soldiers with a club of their own and save many from the grog shops and the brothels. The reestablishment of that part of the exchange would go far to reduce desertion, venereal diseases and alcoholism among our troops."

In 1914 General Pershing was recalled from the Philippine Islands.

His work and that of General Funston was now fully recognized by his countrymen. Peace had come in the Philippines and the victorious leaders had been successful not only with their enemies, but also in winning the confidence of most of the tribes they conquered. It is said there was no man in the islands who was more deeply respected and loved by the natives than was General Pershing. They were fearful of him, also, because they knew that he would do exactly what he said he would do. Strict with

offenders against the laws, he was at the same
time gentle and friendly to the deserving, and
it was not long before all were aware that he
was working not for conquest or for the glory
of his nation, but to help his country solve one
of the most difficult problems left by the Spanish War. That problem was to reconstruct and
reorganize the life among the Filipinos in such
a way that they themselves should be helped
and not hurt by the plan. When General Pershing returned to America, hope was strong
that not many years would elapse before the
little brown men would be able to care for
themselves and be recognized as an independent
nation.

For a brief time he was stationed at the Presidio in San Francisco, California, but soon
afterward was placed in command of the
southwestern division, along the Mexican border. It was while he was stationed there in
command of a scant and greatly extended line,
which required constant change on his own
part in order to keep in touch with the various
elements in his command, that the great

tragedy of the death of his wife and three little daughters occurred.

On August 27, 1915, while he was in command at El Paso, word came to him over the telephone of the awful fire in the Presidio at San Francisco, where his family, then consisting of his wife, three little daughters and a little son, we e residing in his enforced absence. Of these, all except Warren, the little boy, perished in the fire, a maid having succeeded in rescuing the little fellow. When the terrible message was received by the general it is said that at last he inquired, "Is there anything more to be told?"

Upon being assured that he now knew not only the worst but had heard all, he quietly hung up the receiver and turned away. There was to be no manifestation of his almost crushing sorrow. It was his own, and there we too must leave it. There are few who can fail to understand. The lines in his strong face were soon deeper, the graying hair became lighter still, but General Pershing's suffering and sorrow were his own, not even to

116

be referred to except as one of the facts
the life of a man who belongs not to himself
alone, but also to his country.

It has been reported that the general re-
quested that he might be sent on the most
dangerous service to which his country could
assign him. Whether or not he ever made the
request the writer does not know, but that he
might have had such a feeling in his heart can
readily be understood by all. The little
motherless lad, Warren, has been cared for
by the general's sisters, who now reside in
Lincoln, Nebraska.

CHAPTER IX

In Pursuit of Villa

General Pershing had been sent to the Mexican border in command of the Southwestern Division early in 1915. In command of the El Paso patrol district, he necessarily was busy much of his time in guarding and patrolling the long thin lines of our men on duty there.

The troubles with Mexico had been steadily increasing in seriousness. The rivalry and warfare between various leaders in that country had not only brought their own country into a condition of distress, but also had threatened to involve the United States as well. Citizens of the latter country had invested large sums in mining, lumber and other industries in Mexico and were complaining bitterly of the failure of our Government either to protect them or

118

their investments. Again and again, under threats of closing their mines or confiscating their property, they had "bought bonds" of the rival Mexican parties, which was only another name for blackmail.

Raids were becoming increasingly prevalent near the border and already Americans were reported to have been slain by these irresponsible bandits who were loyal only to their leaders and not always to them. The condition was becoming intolerable.

Germany, too, had her agents busy within the borders of Mexico, artfully striving not only to increase her own power in the rich and distracted country, but also to create and foment an unreasonable anger against the United States, vainly hoping in this way to prevent the latter country from entering the World War by compelling her to face these threatening attacks from her neighbor on the south. President Wilson was doing his utmost to hold a steady course through the midst of these perils, which daily were becoming more threatening and perplexing.

The climax came early in March, 1915, when Francesco Villa, the most daring and reckless leader of all the Mexican bandit bands, suddenly with his followers made an attack on the post at Columbus, New Mexico. The American soldiers were taken completely by surprise. Their machine guns (some said there was only one at the post) jammed and their defense was inadequate. They were not prepared. When Villa withdrew he left nine dead civilians and eight dead American soldiers behind him.

Instantly the President decided that the time had come when he must act. There was still the same strong desire to avoid war with Mexico if possible. The same suspicion of Germany was in his mind, but in spite of these things Villa must be punished and Americans must be protected. Quickly a call for regulars and State troops was made and General Pershing was selected as the leader of the punitive expedition.

The New York *Sun*, in an editorial at the time of his selection, said: "At home in the desert country, familiar with the rules of savage warfare, a regular of regulars, sound in judgment as in physique, a born cavalryman, John J. Pershing is an ideal commander for the pursuit into Mexico.''

The selection indeed may have been ''ideal,'' but the conditions confronting the commander were far from sharing in that ideal. Equipment was lacking, many of his men, though they were brave, were untrained, and, most perplexing of all, was the exact relation of Mexico to the United States. There could not be said to exist a state of war and yet no one could say the two countries were at peace. He was invading a hostile country which was not an enemy, for the raids of bandit bands across the border did not mean that Mexico as a state was attacking the United States. He must move swiftly across deserts and through mountain fastnesses, he was denied the use of railroads for transporting either troops or supplies, enemies were on all sides who were familiar with every foot of the region and eager to lure him and his army into traps from which escape would be well nigh impossible. The fact is that for nearly eleven months Pershing maintained his line, extending nearly four hundred miles from his base of supplies, in a country which even if it was not at war was at least hostile. It is not therefore surprising that after his return the State of New Mexico voted a handsome gold medal to the leader of the punitive expedition for his success in an exceedingly difficult task.

It was on the morning of March 15, 1916, when General Pershing dashed across the border in command of ten thousand United States cavalrymen, with orders to "get" Villa. A captain in the Civil War who was in the Battle of Gettysburg, when he learned of the swift advance of General Pershing's forces, said: "The hardest march we ever made was the advance from Frederick. We made thirty miles that day between six o'clock A.M. and eleven o'clock P.M. But Maryland and Pennsylvania are not an alkali desert. I have an idea that twenty-six miles a day, the ground Pershing was covering on that waterless tramp in Mexico, was some hiking." And the advance is one of the marvels of military achievements when it is recalled that the march was begun before either men or supplies, to say nothing of equipment, were in readiness.

It may have been that it was because of his better knowledge of these conditions that the general wrote:

* "Our people are not a warlike people and the average person knows little about our army. The centers of population have never been brought into close contact with it, and, like anything that is unfamiliar, the people entertain a certain prejudice against it. To overcome this prejudice and to arouse and maintain an active interest in military preparedness it will be necessary to adopt some plan that will bring the army more closely in touch with the people. The time for this seems opportune and it can best be done by assigning the various units of the army to prescribed districts for local recruiting.

"If each regiment or smaller unit were composed of young men whose families were neighbors, especially if the home station of that unit were easily accessible, the people would undoubtedly support the unit with men and money. Each regimental unit might be given a local name and there surely would

* Quoted in the *Army and Navy Journal* from the New York *Times*.

be quite as much pride in having a regiment named
for a city or state as in having a war vessel so
named. A regiment recruited locally would start
out with a high *esprit de corps* and the evil of desertion would be eliminated. Men now desert mainly
because they have no pride or interest in the individual organization to which they belong. Local-
ization would soon develop both. It would also in
time become an easy stepping stone to universal
training to which we must come if we are ever to
hope for a satisfactory solution of our military
problem.

"Universal training does not mean that every man
would have to serve with the army two years or
any other given length of time, but it should mean
that every young man though not drawn to the
colors would have to take a certain amount of military training. Universal training is a necessary
prerequisite to effective war armies.

"Under a system of compulsory service the whole
number of men to become eligible each year would
be greater than required for active service in the
army, but selections could be easily determined by
lot. Those not drawn for service with the colors
would be given enough training to teach the meaning of discipline and make them familiar with the
principles of marching, camping and shooting. They
would all be subject to call in case of war and the
question as to whether they were needed at the front
would not be left to the judgment or personal in-

clination of the individual. The humiliating spectacle of expending time and effort after war begins in appealing through the press and platform directly to the people to support the Government would not have to be repeated. Each man would expect to do his part. Men called out for service during the war require at least a year of drill before they are familiar with what the modern soldier must know. The demands of modern warfare upon individuals are greater than ever before and only the thoroughly trained and tried soldier is able to stand the strain. In the Civil War troops were confronted by equally untrained levies.''

Behind this calm, clear and deliberate utterance it is easy to read the unspoken anxiety and the needless strain forced upon the commander of the punitive expedition in pursuit of Villa. And these words were written long before Pershing ever dreamed he would be the leader of a mighty host to cross the seas and in a foreign land fight not only the battles of his country but also those of humanity as well.

Although the punitive expedition failed in its main purpose,—the capture of Villa,—the opinion in America was unanimous that the leadership had been superb. *The American*

Review of Reviews declared that "the expedition was conducted from first to last in a way that reflected credit on American arms."

An interesting incident in this chapter of Pershing's story is that fourteen of the nineteen Apache Indian scouts whom he had helped to capture in the pursuit of Geronimo, in 1886, were aiding him in the pursuit of Villa. Several of these scouts were past seventy years of age; indeed, one was more than eighty, but their keenness on the trail and their long experience made their assistance of great value. One of the best was Sharley and another was Peaches. Several of these Indian scouts are with the colors in France, still with Pershing.

The main facts in the story of the punitive expedition are as follows:

LEADING EVENTS IN THE PUNITIVE EXPEDITION INTO MEXICO

1916

Feb. 17   Report in United States Senate that 76 Americans since 1913 had been killed in Mexico. 36 others had been slain on American soil.

March 9   Villa and his band cross the border and attack the 13th U. S. Cavalry at Columbus, New Mexico. 8 troopers were killed and 9 civilians wounded.

March 10–13   Notes were exchanged between the U. S. and Carranza. The U. S. decided upon an immediate punitive expedition. Two columns estimated at 6,000 men under Brigadier-General John J. Pershing and Colonel Dodd enter Mexico from Columbus and Hachita.

March 20   Three columns are in Mexico. The maximum penetration is reported as 80 miles.

April 11   It was officially announced that 18,000 Americans were now on the border while 12,000 have penetrated 375 miles.

April 16   A false report of Villa's death.

April 23–29   Conferences are held at El Paso between American and Mexican officials. The Americans ask for the active coöperation of the forces of Carranza. Skirmishes are reported in Mexico and raids are made on the frontier by followers of Villa.

May 9   President calls the militia of Texas, New Mexico and Arizona to the border.

	Additional regular troops are also sent.
May 22	Carranza protests to the United States against the violation of Mexican sovereignty.
June 18	President calls many militia units to the federal service for duty on the frontier and in mobilization camps.
June 20	In a note to Carranza the President declines to withdraw American troops.
June 21	A force of Carranza's men attack a scouting body of U. S. cavalry at Carrizal. A score of Americans are killed and 22 made prisoners.
June 22	Secretary of State Lansing informs the governments of South and Central America concerning the intentions of the United States in Mexico.
June 24	Carranza again demands that American troops must not advance west, east or south in Mexico.
June 25	Secretary Lansing enters a demand for the return of the prisoners at Carrizal. In the same letter he also declares that the action at this place was a ''formal avowal of deliberately hostile action.'' He also inquires what Carranza's intentions are.
June 28	Carranza orders the release of the prisoners at Carrizal.

July 1	American troops in Mexico are gradually being withdrawn.
July 4	Carranza suggests the acceptance by the U. S. of Latin-American offers of mediation.
July 7–10	Views of American and Mexican officials are exchanged at Washington. Within three weeks 60,000 militia has been brought to the border.
July 20	Carranza suggests a conference of three commissioners from each nation to confer concerning withdrawal of troops and the raiding of bandits.
July 28	President accepts the proposal.
Aug. 1	The 98,000 militia on the border is increased by 25,000 more.
Aug. 3	Luis Cabrera, Ignacio Bonillas and Alberto J. Pani are selected as Mexican commissioners.
Aug. 22	Franklin K. Lane, George Gray and John R. Mott are named as commissioners of the United States.
Aug. 30	The War Department orders 15,000 militia to return from the border to state mobilization camps.
Sept. 6	American-Mexican joint commission meets at New London, Conn.
Sept 7	The War Department orders a return of militia regiments to be mustered out of federal service.

Sept 22	Militia from Kansas, Wisconsin and Wyoming are ordered to the border in place of the departing units.
Nov. 15	Militia to the number of 5,296 ordered from the border.
Nov. 21	The President's new proposal is placed before the Mexican commissioners.
Nov. 24	At Atlantic City, N. J., a protocol signed by the joint commission is sent to Carranza. It provides for the withdrawal of the punitive expedition from Mexico within 40 days after ratification and also for combined protection for the border.
Dec. 18	Carranza refuses to ratify the protocol and explains his desire to submit a counterstatement. The U. S. force on the border is reduced to 75,000 men, while 12,000 are still in Mexico.
Dec. 27	Carranza asks for revision of the protocol. This is declined by the U. S.

Early in the following year satisfactory adjustments were made and the punitive expedition was withdrawn. Villa was not captured, but it is confidently believed the troubles on the border have been greatly mitigated.

CHAPTER X

CALLED TO COMMAND THE AMERICAN EXPEDITIONARY FORCES IN FRANCE

MEANWHILE matters were moving swiftly, the results of which were to summon General Pershing to other and far higher duties. The attitude of Germany was steadily becoming too unbearable for any self-respecting nation to endure. War may be the great evil which it is often called, and doubtless no words can describe its horrors, but there is one evil even worse—for a nation to lose its ideals. The time for action by the United States had come.

In President Wilson's war message after referring to the dastardly deeds of Germany he wrote, "I was for a little while unable to believe that such things would be done by any government that had hitherto subscribed to humane practices of civilized nations," and he refers also to the wanton and wholesale destruction of the lives of noncombatants—men, women and children—engaged in pursuits "which have always, even in the darkest periods of modern history, been deemed innocent and legitimate."

In spite of the Teutonic claim of a higher "kultur" than other nations and the loudly expressed desires for the "freedom of the seas," Germany's brutal disregard of the rights of neutrals had extended far beyond the confines of Belgium, which she ruthlessly invaded and ravaged.

On the sea her former promises were like her treaty with Belgium—"scraps of paper."

And the President had now behind him not merely the sentiment of his people, but also specific examples to uphold him. For instance, Admiral Sampson in the war with Spain, had appeared May 12, 1898, with his fleet before Santiago, Cuba. There he conducted a reconnoissance in force in his efforts to locate the Spanish fleet, of which Admiral Cervera was in command. Sampson, however, did not bombard the city, because, in accordance with the accepted laws of nations, he would have been required to give due notice of his intention in order that the sick, women, children and non-combatants might be removed. And yet everyone knew that a hard, quick bombardment of Santiago would have given him the city. He attacked the forts only, and before a gun was fired gave his ships' captains word that they were to avoid hitting the Spanish Military Hospital.

Even in the general orders of the German Admiralty staff (Berlin, June 22, 1914) was the following direction, after stating that the passengers of every armed captured merchant vessel were to be left to go free "unless it appears they have participated in the resistance": "Before proceeding to the destruction of the (neutral) vessel (which has been seized for proper reason), the safety of all persons on board, and, so far as possible their effects, is to be provided for."

President Wilson, at first unable to believe that Germany was deliberately violating her word and even after it was impossible to avoid the conclusion that the campaign of the Teutons was being conducted, to use their own expression, "ruthlessly," still was doing his utmost to keep the United States out of the World War. For this he was bitterly assailed and criticised. However, he patiently held to his policy announced a year before, that he would "wait until facts become unmistakable and even susceptible of only one interpretation."

As early as December 24, 1914, Admiral Von Tirpitz in numerous inspired newspaper articles and interviews, began to explain the possibility of a very decided change in the German U-boat campaign. This too was before Germany was really suffering in any marked degree from the tightening work of the British navy. In spite of his arrogant words, however, the German admiral directly asks, "What will America say?"

On February 4, 1915, the Germans in a way that was outside all international law, publicly declared that 'within certain expressed limits of the sea or war zone, their U-boats would sink vessels without warning found there without permission, or if they were engaged in dealings with the enemy.'

Six days later President Wilson warned Germany that she will be held to "strict accountability" if the rights of American vessels within the proscribed limits are violated.

It was April 22, 1915, when, through the acknowledged direction of the German Embassy, advertisements appeared in New York papers warning all against sailing on vessels planning to pass through the war zone. And this was done in the face of the President's words and the correspondence that had been carried on between the two countries.

The *Lusitania* was sunk May 7, 1915. A thousand lives were lost, many of them Americans. A roar of anger rose from America and the civilized world at the brutality of this act, as well as at the dastardly disregard of the rights of neutral nations. "They were warned," said the Germans glibly, as if their "warning" was sufficient. For a nation that had made huge profits in selling munitions at other times to warring peoples their "warning" would have been ridiculous had it not been tragic. The commander of the U-boat received a German medal for his "gallantry" in sinking the *Lusitania* and sending hundreds of innocent victims to their watery graves. As if to add insult to injury Germany proclaimed a holiday for her schools on the occasion.

President Wilson still held to his patient course. He would give Germany every opportunity to explain the act before he himself acted. May 13, 1915, his first so-called *"Lusitania* letter" was written. Germany replied May 28th, declaring that she was justified in sinking the great vessel. On June 9th, the President sent his "second *Lusitania* letter," and correspondence followed which plainly indicated that Germany was trying to evade the real issue.

July 31, 1915, saw the "third *Lusitania* letter," for even then the President was doing his utmost to avoid war, if avoidance was possible. On August 19, 1915, the *Arabic* was torpedoed by a U-boat and still other Americans lost their lives. The German ambassador to the

United States, Count von Bernstorff, however, apparently thought to stave off action by pledging (orally) for his country that her submarines would not sink "liners" without warning.

The ambassador's words were not unlike those previously received, for instead of the matter being settled, still more unsatisfactory correspondence followed and other boats also were sent to the bottom of the sea.

The following February, Germany made certain proposals that had an appearance of a grudging or compulsory willingness on her part to provide for the *Lusitania* victims, but within a few days (March 24, 1916), another passenger steamer, the *Sussex*, was torpedoed, and among the lost were Americans.

The feeling in Washington was becoming tense and was still more intensified in April, when Germany sneeringly explained that she was not positive whether or not she sank the *Sussex*. She did admit, however, that one of her submarines had been in action near the place where the *Sussex* was sent to the bottom.

Eight days later President Wilson threatened

Germany that he would break off diplomatic relations if similar acts recurred. Perhaps because she was biding her time Germany on May 4th gave a "promise" that no more ships should be sunk without warning.

In October of that same year (1916) a German submarine appeared off the New England coast. Her officers put into Newport and it is said were even graciously received and most courteously treated. Then, in return for the hospitality thus received, the submarine sank the *Stephano*, which had a large body of Americans on board returning from a vacation spent in Newfoundland. Without doubt many would have been lost if American men-of-war had not been at hand to rescue the victims from the water. Still, apparently there was not even a thought in the minds of Germany's rulers, that they had violated any rules of decency, to say nothing of rules of right.

The patience of the United States was near the breaking point when still the dastardly deeds did not cease, and few were surprised when at last, January 31, 1917, Germany discovered that deceit no longer was possible and that the patience and hope of America could no longer be abused. On that date the German leaders came out openly and informed the President that they planned to "begin an unrestricted submarine war." Three days afterward President Wilson gave the German ambassador to the United States his passports and recalled the American ambassador (Gerard) from Berlin.

Such evasion and hypocrisy, such wanton brutality and cruelty as had been displayed by Germany were without parallel in history—or at least since the history of civilization began. Naturally a declaration of war by the United States was the only possible outcome.

The unlawful sinking of American vessels or of other vessels having Americans on board makes up a list that is striking when it is looked at as a whole and it is recalled that they had been sunk after Germany had "ruthlessly" repudiated the pledges she had given.

Housatonic, February 3, 1917.
Lyman M. Law, February 13, 1917.

Algonquin, March 2, 1917.
Vigilancia, March 16, 1917.
City of Memphis, March 17, 1917.
Illinois, March 17, 1917.
Healdton, March 21, 1917 (sunk outside the "prohibited zone" arbitrarily proclaimed by Germany).
Aztec, April 1, 1917.

Perhaps in this list should also be included the sinking of the *William P. Frye,* January 28, 1915, by the German raider, *Prinz Eitel Friedrich.* The very acme of impudence seems to have been reached when this raider, after having unlawfully sunk American vessels, sought refuge in the American port of Newport News, Virginia. No clearer testimony has ever been given of the state of mind among the Germans, unless it is the actions of the German crew of this vessel after they had been interned.

Preceding the declaration of war by the United States, two hundred and twenty-six of her citizens had lost their lives by the unlawful acts of German submarines. Among those who perished in this manner were many women and children. In nearly every instance there was not even the form of an excuse that Germany was acting in accord with the laws of nations. Outside the American vessels the official estimate made at that time by the Government of the United States was that six hundred and sixty-eight vessels of neutral nations had been sunk by the piratical German submarines. It appeared almost as if the rulers of Germany either were insane or were so bent on their wild dreams of subduing the world to their will that they deliberately said to themselves, "evil, be thou our good." They had thrown down the gauntlet to the civilized parts of the entire world. Even after Brazil, China, Bolivia, Guatemala and other nations broke off diplomatic relations with Germany and almost all the civilized nations of the earth had protested against the brutal policy boldly followed by her, she whiningly complained that the world was jealous of her greatness and had combined to overthrow the "kultur" she was so eager to share with all mankind.

In addition to the frightfulness of Germany on the seas (a term she herself had invented and blatantly advocated), the activity of German spies and the dangerous "propaganda" she was putting forth in the United States were even more insulting and quite as threatening to American lives and property as was her dastardly work with her submarines. Many of the intrigues were not made known by the Government of the United States.

When the message of President Wilson was presented, the committee on Foreign Affairs in the House of Representatives went on formal record, after presenting its resolution declaring a state of war to exist between the United States and Germany, that within our country at least twenty-one crimes or "unfriendly" acts had been committed either by the direction of or connivance with the Imperial German Government. And nearly every one of these unfriendly acts in itself was a sufficient basis for war. Included in this list were the following clearly known facts:

An office had been maintained in the United

States to issue fraudulent passports for German reservists. This work was under the direction of Captain von Papen, who was a member of the German Embassy.

German spies were sent to England who were supplied with passports from the United States.

In defiance of our laws steamers had been sent from our ports with supplies for German sea raiders.

Hindus within the United States had been supplied with money by Germany to stir up revolutions and revolts in India.

A German agent had been sent from the United States to blow up with dynamite the international bridge at Vanceboro, Maine.

Germany had provided funds for her agents in the United States to blow up factories in Canada.

Five distinct conspiracies had been unearthed, in which Germany was the guiding spirit, to make and place bombs on ships leaving ports of the United States. Several of those conspiracies were successful and the murderous bombs were placed even on board vessels of the United States. She was working to arouse and increase a feeling of bitterness in Mexico against the United States. In this way it was hoped by Germany that we would be drawn into war with Mexico, and thereby be prevented from entering into either the Great War or European affairs.

Providing huge sums of money to be used in bribing newspapers in the United States to publish articles which should prevent America from entering the war and arouse a feeling of bitterness against England and France. Later it was admitted by German agents that a plan had been formed by which forty leading American newspapers were to be purchased and used for this purpose. The plan was not wholly successful, but many papers or certain editors were proved to have been bought with this end in view and some fully earned their money.

Insult was added to injury. Such colossal brutality was even commended and upheld by the friends of Germany and defended on the ground that the "fatherland" had been attacked treacherously and therefore was entitled, whether or not she was acting in accord with established and accepted laws, to which she had given her approval, to defend herself in every possible way.

Perhaps the climax of this outrageous disregard of decency came when Secretary Lansing exposed March 1, 1917, the infamous "Zimmerman note." It was written before war had been declared, and, officially at least, Germany and the United States were friends at the time. Indeed it was only three days after the appearance of President Wilson before the Senate with his plan for a league of nations to secure and assure justice and peace for all nations. This infamous note was even brought to the United States and was to be carried across the border into Mexico, a country with which we were not at war and with which the President was doing his utmost to maintain peace.

It is impossible to give the entire message but the following extracts will reveal its character:

"Berlin, January 19, 1917.

"On February 1 we intend to begin submarine war unrestricted. In spite of this it is our intention to keep neutral the United States of America.

"If this attempt is not successful we propose an alliance on the following basis with Mexico,—That we shall make war together and together make peace. We shall give general financial support and it is understood that Mexico is to reconquer the lost territory in New Mexico, Texas and Arizona. The details are left to you for settlement."

The German Secretary then goes on to instruct the German Minister in Mexico to open secret negotiations with Carranza just as soon as it is plain that the proposed U-boat campaign brings the United States into the war and also to get Carranza to draw Japan into the proposed war against us.

Just how the Government obtained this note will not be known until an explanation is given later, but its authorized publication by Secretary Lansing instantly aroused an intense feeling of anger throughout the country. For a "friendly" nation to be plotting against a "friend," to attempt to use that nation even

CHAPTER XI

WHY AMERICA WENT TO WAR WITH GERMANY

A STATE of war had been declared April 5, 1917, to exist between the United States and the Imperial German Government. There is no clearer or more forceful statement of the reason why we went to war than the address delivered by President Wilson at Washington on Flag Day, June 14, 1917:

MY FELLOW-CITIZENS: We meet to celebrate Flag Day because this flag which we honor and under which we serve is the emblem of our unity, our power, our thought and purpose as a nation. It has no other character than that which we give it from generation to generation. The choices are ours. It floats in majestic silence above the hosts that execute those choices, whether in peace or in war. And yet, though silent, it speaks to us—speaks to us of the past, of the men and women who went before us and of the records they wrote upon it. We cele-

149

brate the day of its birth; and from its birth until now it has witnessed a great history, has floated on high the symbol of great events, of a great plan of life worked out by a great people. We are about to carry it into battle, to lift it where it will draw the fire of our enemies. We are about to bid thousands, hundreds of thousands, it may be millions, of our men, the young, the strong, the capable men of the nation, to go forth and die beneath it on fields of blood far away—for what? For some unaccustomed thing? For something for which it has never sought the fire before? American armies were never before sent across the seas. Why are they sent now? For some new purpose, for which this great flag has never been carried before, or for some old, familiar, heroic purpose for which it has seen men, its own men, die on every battlefield upon which Americans have borne arms since the Revolution?

These are questions which must be answered. We are Americans. We in our turn serve America, and can serve her with no private purpose. We must use her flag as she has always used it. We are accountable at the bar of history and must plead in utter frankness what purpose it is we seek to serve.

FORCED INTO WAR

It is plain enough how we were forced into the war. The extraordinary insults and aggressions of the Imperial German Government left us no self-respecting choice but to take up arms in defense of our rights as a free people and of our honor as a sovereign Government. The military masters of Germany denied us the right to be neutral. They filled our unsuspecting communities with vicious spies and conspirators and sought to corrupt the opinion of our people in their own behalf. When they found that they could not do that, their agents diligently spread sedition among us and sought to draw our own citizens from their allegiance—and some of those agents were men connected with the official embassy of the German Government itself here in our own capital. They sought by violence to destroy our industries and arrest our commerce. They tried to incite Mexico to take up arms against us and to draw Japan into a hostile alliance with her—and that, not by indirection, but by direct suggestion from the Foreign Office in Berlin. They impudently denied us the use of the high seas and repeatedly executed their threat that they would send to their death any of our people who ventured to approach the coasts of Europe. And many of our own people were corrupted. Men began to look upon their own neighbors with suspicion and to wonder in their hot resentment and surprise whether there was any community in which hostile intrigue did not lurk. What great nation in such circumstances would not have taken up arms? Much as we had desired peace, it was denied us, and not of our own choice. This flag under which we serve would have been dishonored had we withheld our hand.

But that is only part of the story. We know now as clearly as we knew before we were ourselves engaged that we are not the enemies of the German people and that they are not our enemies. They did not originate or desire this hideous war or wish that we should be drawn into it; and we are vaguely conscious that we are fighting their cause, as they will some day see it, as well as our own. They are themselves in the grip of the same sinister power that has now at last stretched its ugly talons out and drawn blood from us. The whole world is at war because the whole world is in the grip of that power and is trying out the great battle which shall determine whether it is to be brought under its mastery or fling itself free.

THE MASTERS OF GERMANY

The war was begun by the military masters of Germany, who proved to be also the masters of Austria-Hungary. These men have never regarded nations as peoples, men, women, and children of like blood and frame as themselves, for whom Governments existed and in whom Governments had their life. They have regarded them merely as serviceable organizations which they could by force or intrigue bend or corrupt to their own purpose. They have regarded the smaller States, in particular, and the peoples who could be overwhelmed by force as

their natural tools and instruments of domination.
Their purpose has long been avowed. The statesmen of other nations, to whom that purpose was
incredible, paid little attention; regarded what German professors expounded in their classrooms and
German writers set forth to the world as the goal
of German policy, as rather the dream of minds de-
tached from practical affairs, as preposterous private
conceptions of German destiny, than as the actual
plans of responsible rulers; but the rulers of Germany themselves knew all the while what concrete
plans, what well-advanced intrigues lay back of what
the professors and the writers were saying, and were
glad to go forward unmolested, filling the thrones
of Balkan States with German Princes, putting
German officers at the service of Turkey to drill
her armies and make interest with her Government,
developing plans of sedition and rebellion in India
and Egypt, setting their fires in Persia. The demands made by Austria upon Serbia were a mere
single step in a plan which compassed Europe and
Asia, from Berlin to Bagdad. They hoped those demands might not arouse Europe, but they meant to
press them whether they did or not, for they thought
themselves ready for the final issue of arms.

A TOOL OF GERMANY

Their plan was to throw a broad belt of German
military power and political control across the very
center of Europe and beyond the Mediterranean into

the heart of Asia; and Austria-Hungary was to be as much their tool and pawn as Serbia or Bulgaria or Turkey or the ponderous States of the East. Austria-Hungary, indeed, was to become part of the Central German Empire, absorbed and dominated by the same forces and influences that had originally cemented the German States themselves. The dream had its heart at Berlin. It could have had a heart nowhere else! It rejected the idea of solidarity of race entirely. The choice of peoples played no part in it at all. It contemplated binding together racial and political units which could be kept together only by force—Czechs, Magyars, Croats, Serbs, Rumanians, Turks, Armenians—the proud States of Bohemia and Hungary, the stout little commonwealths of the Balkans, the indomitable Turks, the subtle peoples of the East. These peoples did not wish to be united. They ardently desired to direct their own affairs, would be satisfied only by undisputed independence. They could be kept quiet only by the presence of the constant threat of armed men. They would live under a common power only by sheer compulsion and await the day of revolution. But the German military statesmen had reckoned with all that and were ready to deal with it in their own way.

THE PRESENT CONDITION

And they have actually carried the greater part of that amazing plan into execution. Look how

154

things stand. Austria is at their mercy. It has acted, not upon its own initiative nor upon the choice of its own people, but at Berlin's dictation ever since the war began. Its people now desire peace, but cannot have it until leave is granted from Berlin. The so-called Central Powers are in fact but a single power. Serbia is at its mercy, should its hands be but for a moment freed; Bulgaria has consented to its will and Rumania is overrun. The Turkish armies, which Germans trained, are serving Germany, certainly not themselves, and the guns of German warships lying in the harbor at Constantinople remind Turkish statesmen every day that they have no choice but to take their orders from Berlin. From Hamburg to the Persian Gulf the net is spread.

A FALSE CRY FOR PEACE

Is it not easy to understand the eagerness for peace that has been manifested from Berlin ever since the snare was set and sprung? Peace, peace, peace has been the talk of her Foreign Office now for a year or more; not peace upon her own initiative, but upon the initiative of the nations over which she now deems herself to hold the advantage. A little of the talk has been public, but most of it has been private. Through all sorts of channels it has come to me, and in all sorts of guises, but never with the terms disclosed which the German Government would be willing to accept. That Government

155

has other valuable pawns in its hands besides those I have mentioned. It still holds a valuable part of France, though with slowly relaxing grasp, and practically the whole of Belgium. Its armies press close upon Russia and overrun Poland at their will. It cannot go further; it dare not go back. It wishes to close its bargain before it is too late, and it has little left to offer for the pound of flesh it will demand.

The military masters under whom Germany is bleeding see very clearly to what point fate has brought them. If they fall back or are forced back an inch their power both abroad and at home will fall to pieces like a house of cards. It is their power at home they are thinking about now more than their power abroad. It is that power which is trembling under their very feet; and deep fear has entered their hearts. They have but one chance to perpetuate their military power or even their controlling political influence. If they can secure peace now with the immense advantages still in their hands, which they have up to this point apparently gained, they will have justified themselves before the German people; they will have gained by force what they promised to gain by it—an immense expansion of German power, an immense enlargement of German industrial and commercial opportunities. Their prestige will be secure, and with their prestige their political power. If they fail, their people will thrust them aside; a Government accountable to the people themselves will be set up in Germany as it has been in England, in the United States, in France, and in all the great countries of the modern time except Germany. If they succeed they are safe and Germany and the world are undone; if they fail Germany is saved and the world will be at peace. If they succeed America will fall within the menace. We and all the rest of the world must remain armed, as they will remain, and must make ready for the next step in their aggression; if they fail the world may unite for peace and Germany may be of the union.

Do you not now understand the new intrigue, the intrigue for peace, and why the masters of Germany do not hesitate to use any agency that promises to effect their purpose, the deception of the nations? Their present particular aim is to deceive all those who throughout the world stand for the rights of peoples and the self-government of nations; for they see what immense strength the forces of justice and of liberalism are gathering out of this war.

PROPAGANDA

They are employing liberals in their enterprise. They are using men, in Germany and without, as their spokesmen whom they have hitherto despised and oppressed, using them for their own destruction —Socialists, the leaders of labor, the thinkers they have hitherto sought to silence. Let them once succeed and these men, now their tools, will be ground to powder beneath the weight of the great military empire they will have set up; the revolutionists in Russia will be cut off from all succor or cooperation in Western Europe and a counter-revolution fostered and supported; Germany herself will lose her chance of freedom, and all Europe will arm for the next, the final, struggle.

The sinister intrigue is being no less actively conducted in this country than in Russia and in every country in Europe to which the agents and dupes of the Imperial German Government can get access. That Government has many spokesmen here, in places high and low. They have learned discretion. They keep within the law. It is opinion they utter now, not sedition. They proclaim the liberal purposes of their masters; declare this a foreign war which can touch America with no danger to either her lands or her institutions; set England at the center of the stage and talk of her ambition to assert economic dominion throughout the world; appeal to our ancient tradition of isolation in the politics of the nations, and seek to undermine the Government with false professions of loyalty to its principles.

But they will make no headway. The false betray themselves always in every accent. It is only friends and partisans of the German Government whom we have already identified who utter these thinly disguised disloyalties. The facts are patent to all the world, and nowhere are they more plainly seen than in the United States, where we are accustomed to deal with facts and not with sophistries; and the great fact that stands out above all the rest is that this is a people's war, a war for freedom and justice and self-government among all the nations of the world, a war to make the world safe for the peoples who live upon it and have made it their own, the German people themselves included; and that with us rests the choice to break through all these hypocrisies and patent cheats and masks of brute force and help set the world free, or else stand aside and let it be dominated a long age through by sheer weight of arms and the arbitrary choices of self-constituted masters, by the nation which can maintain the biggest armies and the most irresistible armaments—a power to which the world has afforded no parallel and in the face of which political freedom must wither and perish.

For us there is but one choice. We have made it. Woe be to the man or group of men that seeks to stand in our way in this day of high resolution when every principle we hold dearest is to be vindicated and made secure for the salvation of the nations. We are ready to plead at the bar of history, and our flag shall wear a new luster. Once more we shall make good with our lives and fortunes the great faith to which we were born, and a new glory shall shine in the face of our people.

The war was now on. All the latent power of the nation of every kind was to be used in every way to help drive the German menace from the world. A visit to the new world by Marshal Joffre, Viviani, Lord Asquith and others helped to accelerate matters. No one will know until the war is ended just what took place in the councils between these great men of the old world and the leaders of the new.

Everyone does know, however, the instantaneous activity and enthusiasm which seized with compelling force upon the people of the United States.

But there must be a military leader. What was more natural than that the choice should fall upon General John Joseph Pershing? General Funston had died suddenly at San Antonio, Texas, and there was no one now to outrank the leader of the punitive expedition into Mexico.

So General Pershing was selected. The man who had feared he was to be ignored and left forgotten in the jungles of the Philippines was now to be the Commander of the American Expeditionary Force in France. Promotion once more had come to the man who had sought first to be worthy to be promoted.

CHAPTER XII

IN ENGLAND AND FRANCE

ON June 8, 1917, General Pershing with his
staff arrived (on the White Star Liner, *Baltic*),
at Liverpool. There was keen excitement in
the busy city and a warm welcome for the
military representative of the great republic
which now was one of the Allies. Accompanied
by a guard of honor and a military band which
was playing the Star Spangled Banner, a
British general was waiting to pay due honor
to the arriving military leader. The British
admiral in command at Liverpool was also
present to greet the arriving General, as was
also the Lord Mayor of the city. The docks
and shops, the houses and parks were filled
with a waiting, eager throng that was quiet in
its deep, tense feeling.

161

To the British public General Pershing gave out the following message:

"We are very proud and glad to be the standard bearers of our country in this great war for civilization and to land on British soil. The welcome which we have received is magnificent and deeply appreciated. We hope in time to be playing our part—and we hope it will be a big part—on the western front."

As soon as the American Commander had been suitably greeted he started for London by special train. The official state car had been attached to the train for the General's benefit. In his swift ride through the many busy cities which remind one more of American cities than does any other part of England, through the beautiful and carefully cultivated rural regions, past Oxford with its crowning towers, many hoary with age, the party was taken. It is only natural to conjecture what thoughts must have been in the mind of the General at the time. Was he thinking of Laclede and the negro school which he had taught? Or of his modestly brave work in Cuba and the Philippines? Or did the statement he had made to a friend years before when he started for West Point that "war was no more and a gun would not be fired in a hundred years," again come back to him, when, seated in the car of state, he was swept swiftly toward London on that beautiful and historic day in June?

In London, United States Ambassador Page, Admiral Sims of the United States Navy, Lord Derby, British Secretary of State for War, General Lord French and many other leaders of the British Army were waiting to receive him. Throngs of people on every side were doing their utmost to show that they too as well as the representatives of their Government, wanted to manifest their appreciation in every possible way of the coming of the Commander of the American Expeditionary Force.

The following day General Pershing was presented formally to King George V at Buckingham Palace. General Lord Brooke, commander of the Twelfth Canadian Infantry Brigade, as was most fitting, was the spokesman. To General Pershing the King said:

"It has been the dream of my life to see the two great English-speaking nations more closely united. My dreams have been realized. It is with the utmost pleasure that I welcome you, at the head of the American contingent, to our shores."

His Majesty conversed informally with each member of the General's staff and talked with the General a longer time. His intense interest and enthusiasm as well as his gratitude were manifest not only in his spoken words but also in the cordial grasp of his hand when they departed. It was the representative of one great nation trying to express his appreciation to the representative of another nation.

There were numerous formal calls and entertainments to follow and on June 11th, when these all had been duly done, General Pershing and Ambassador Page were entertained at luncheon by King George and Queen Mary, who personally showed their guests through the historic rooms and beautiful grounds of the palace. It was not merely a meeting of the English king and the American soldier—it was the quiet manifestation of the deep feeling and strong ties that now bound together the two great peoples they represented.

General Pershing then departed for the War Office where already members of his staff had been busily conferring with the corresponding members of the British Army.

In the afternoon of that busy day General Pershing was taken as a visitor to the House of Commons. In the Distinguished Visitors Gallery he sat watching the scene before him though he himself in reality was the observed of all the observers, as perhaps he was made aware a little later when as a guest of the members he "took tea" on the Terrace.

In the evening he was the guest of Ambassador Page at dinner when among others he met Premier Lloyd George, Arthur J. Balfour, Lord Derby, Lord Robert Cecil, Viscount French, Admiral Sir John Jellicoe, Vice-Admiral William S. Sims, U. S. N., and General Jan Smuts. It may all have been a part of the formal reception of a welcome visitor, but it also was more, for in this way England and America were doing their utmost to express to the world the cordial relations existing between the two great nations now banded together to fight a common foe.

There are many formalities which have grown to be a part of the reception of the representative of a foreign power by the country which receives him. In a democratic land, like the United States these may appear to be somewhat exaggerated, but they have also become the expression of the desire to honor the land from which the visitor comes and consequently cannot be ignored. Shaking hands as an expression of personal regard is doubtless a somewhat meaningless conventionality, but the man who refuses to shake hands is looked upon as a boor. Doubtless General Pershing, whatever his simpler tastes might have dictated, was well aware that behind all the formal display was the deep-seated desire to honor the country whose personal representative he was.

After a visit to a training camp to witness the British method of training for fighting in the trenches, he was the guest at a luncheon of Lord Derby, the British Secretary of State for War. Although the day had been strenuous, nevertheless in the evening he and eighteen members of his staff were the guests of the British Government at a formal war-dinner. This dinner was served at Lancaster House, a beautiful building which the Government uses solely for state entertainment of distinguished visitors from abroad. Eight members of the British Cabinet were among the thirty present. The dinner was served in the magnificiently furnished dining-hall. The guests were seated at six round tables, each presided over by one of the distinguished men of Great Britain, the Prime Minister sitting at the head of the first table and Lord Curzon, Lord President of the Council; the Right Honorable George M. Barnes, Pensions Minister; Viscount Milner, member of the War Cabinet; Earl of Derby, Secretary for War and Sir Alfred Mond, presiding at the others.

The four days of formal welcome in England were at last ended and General Pershing and his staff sailed for France where the military activities of the United States were to be made a part of the common purpose to turn Germany back from her designs.

In France, too, although she is not a kingdom, there were to be certain formal ceremonies of recognition. The French people are somewhat more demonstrative than the English, but behind it all was the common enthusiasm over the entrance of America into the Great War.

Of General Pershing's reception at Boulogne we have already learned.* Before he departed for Paris, however, he said to the reporters of the French newspapers, whom he received in the private car which the French Government had provided for his use: "The reception we have received is of great significance. .It has impressed us greatly. It means that from the present moment our aims are the same."

To the representatives of the American press, whom he welcomed after he had received the French, he said: "America has entered this war with the fullest intention of doing her

* See Chapter I.
168

share, no matter how great or how small that share may be. Our allies can depend on that.''

Great crowds of enthusiastic people from streets, walls, windows and housetops greeted the American General when the train that was bringing him entered the Gare du Nord at Paris. Cordons of "blue devils" were on the platforms of the station and dense lines of troops patrolled the streets and guarded adjacent blocks as the party was escorted to the Place de la Concorde, where General Pershing was to make his temporary headquarters at the Hotel de Crillon.

Bands were playing the Star Spangled Banner and the Marseillaise, the flag of the United States was waving in thousands of hands and displayed from almost every building, while a steady shout like the roar of the ocean, "Vive l'Amerique!" greeted the party as the automobiles in which they were riding advanced along the densely packed streets. It is said that General Pershing was "visibly affected" by the ovation into which his welcome had been turned. What a contrast it all was to the life and work in the jungles of the Philippines where the young officer had perhaps feared he had been left and forgotten. And yet it was the faithful, persistent, honest work done for the little brown Moro people which helped to make the present occasion possible.

In the evening of that day (June 13th) American Ambassador Sharp gave a dinner in honor of the coming of General Pershing. At this dinner the chief officers of the French army and navy were present. Indeed in the brief time before General Pershing was to assume his active duties it almost seemed as if the desire of the French Government and the French people to do honor to the American commander would test his powers of endurance to the uttermost. There were several events, however, that stand out in the foreground of those remarkable days.

CHAPTER XIII

At the Tomb of Napoleon

One of these notable events was the visit of General Pershing to the Hotel des Invalides in which is the tomb of the most brilliant soldier of all history—Napoleon Bonaparte. General Galterre and General Niox, the latter in charge of the famous monument, received the American General and his staff when they arrived at the marvelous building.

An interesting incident that was reported as having occurred directly after the entrance of the party was the spontaneous action of General Pershing, when his party met some of the aged veterans of the former wars of the French. Impulsively stopping when he was saluted by a bent and aged soldier who had seen service in the Crimean War, General Pershing shook the old soldier by his hand as he said, "It is a great honor for a young soldier like myself to press the hand of an old soldier like yourself who has seen such glorious service." This natural and impulsive action by the American is said to have deeply touched not only the Crimean veteran, but also all who saw it and even more those who later heard of it, for the simple act was soon a topic of conversation among the already deeply enthused people of Paris.

The American soldiers were conducted first to the great rotunda where one can stand, and, looking down, see the tomb of Napoleon resting in eloquent silence in the sarcophagus beneath. But the Commander of the American Expeditionary forces was to have a still more distinctive honor—he was to be taken into the crypt itself. How much of an honor the French consider this may be judged from the fact that in addition to the crowned heads of Europe that had been admitted there, Ex-President Theodore Roosevelt is the only other American previously taken to this spot. It was also a part of the directions which Napoleon himself had left that only a Marshal of France was to remain uncovered in the presence of the Little Corporal of Corsica.

Naturally the American soldiers followed this precedent and it was Marshal Joffre himself who led them to the crypt. The door is immense and heavy, and made of brass. Just before the great key was inserted in the lock and the massive door was slowly to swing open, Marshal Joffre and General Niox left General Pershing alone before it. Those who saw him report that General Pershing drew a deep breath and then without confusion or delay quickly turned the key in the lock of the great brass door.

In a small alcove within the crypt was the case which held Napoleon's sword. General Niox quietly unlocked this case and took out the famous sword and kissed it. Then he extended the sword to the American soldier. General Pershing received the weapon, for an instant held it at salute and then he too kissed the hilt. One cannot help wondering whether the impressive moment suggested to the General the mighty contrast between the aims of Napoleon and those which were guiding the United States in the desperate war in which she now was to share. Brilliant as Napoleon was, mighty strategist and soldier that he proved himself to be, it is difficult even for his warmest admirers to defend the principles (or explain the lack of them) that controlled him in his campaigns. On the other hand, Pershing was the representative of a nation which was to fight with its utmost power—not for conquest nor to overthrow its rivals. Vast sums were to be expended, millions of men were to respond to the call to the colors—for what? "To make the world a decent place to live in." The living and the dead met in the crypt of the Hotel des Invalides, but the aims that animated the two men—one in the early days of the preceding century, and the other in the year 1917—were as far removed from each other as the East is from the West.

A ceremony like that with which Napoleon's sword had been extended to General Pershing was also followed in the case of the cross of

174

the Legion of Honor, the visitor holding it to his lips a moment and then passing it back to General Niox. A correspondent writing of the occasion says: "This was the most signal honor France ever bestowed upon any man. Before this occasion not even a Frenchman was permitted to hold the sacred relics in his hands. Kings and princes have been taken to the crypt that holds the body of the great Emperor, but they only viewed the sword and cross through the plate glass of the case in which they rested. The relics had not been touched since the time of Louis Philippe."

Next followed a formal call upon the American ambassador and then with lines of soldiers and the music of many military bands he was escorted to Elysée Palace, where formally he was to be presented to President Poincaré. Still the enthusiasm of the people endeavored to find expression. Flags and cheers were on every side. Flowers were cast upon the slowly advancing procession and there were many eager watchers, young and old alike, down whose cheeks unchecked tears were falling. The occasion was formal and stately, but its necessary formalities were not able to repress the deep emotions of the brave and valiant people.

Instead of the enthusiasm dying away it almost seemed as if it had increased in volume when General Pershing entered the diplomatic box that afternoon in the Chamber of Deputies. Premier Ribot was addressing the body when the General quietly and without any ostentation took the seat assigned him.

Speedily, however, the arrival of the American General became known in the chamber. The deputies leaped to their feet and cheered and then remained standing and continued their cheering. General Pershing was at last compelled to rise and bow to the assembly in acknowledgment of the remarkable greeting which he had received. Then the packed galleries took up the same theme. "Vive l'Amerique!" resounded loud and long and then was repeated again and again, as if the grateful spectators were fearful lest their former attempts to express their feelings had not been adequate. And all this applause was against every tradition and custom of the dignified Chamber of Deputies.

At last it was possible for the Premier to continue his address, but no longer was he speaking of Greece, as he had been when the Americans had entered, he now was doing his utmost to portray the might and the unselfish devotion of the nation across the sea whose leading soldier was now not only with them in soul, but also in body. He closed his eloquent address by quoting the words of President Wilson, "The day has come to conquer or submit. We will not submit; we will vanquish."

M. Viviani, who recently had visited the United States, was the speaker to follow the Premier. Eloquent, earnest, devoted—there is no one to whose words the Chamber usually is more willing to listen. Viviani at this time also spoke of the United States—its people, its President, its Army and its help, enlarging particularly on the principles for which both France and America were fighting.

When the eloquent speaker ended his address, almost as if the impulse had been kept too long under control, the Deputies again rose and cheered and continued their cheering for General Pershing, until at last once more he was compelled to rise and bow in his acknowledgment of the remarkable ovation he had received. And the cheers continued after he had gone.

Before the people of Paris, Joffre and Pershing stood together, each bare-headed, on the morning of June 15th. They were on the balcony of the Military Club. In the Place de l'Opera was a crowd assembled to do honor to the two military leaders—a public reception by the city. The wild cheering rose in waves. The excitement was intense. The hopes of the people, who, as one distinguished Frenchman said, "had surprised not only the world, but also their own nation by their bravery, determination and heroic endurance," were now keyed to the highest pitch. America was coming. Nay, America is here in the person of its commander, whose Alsatian ancestors years before had found a home in America. Surely the peoples were indeed one. "Vive l'Amerique!" "Vive Joffre!" "Vive Pershing!" It almost seemed as if the cheering would never stop.

A correspondent describes what occurred in a momentary lull in the tumult. A young girl, excited, ardent, patriotic, in a clear call, was distinctly heard above the cries of the vast assembly as she shouted, "Vive Joffre, who saved us from defeat! Vive Pershing, who brings us victory!"

Instantly the crowd responded and for a moment it seemed as if the excitement would break all bounds. The applause became deafening. The vast assemblage took up the moving words of the unknown young girl. "Vive Joffre!" "Vive Pershing!" rose in a wild cry of joy and hope. Indeed, long after the two soldiers had withdrawn and the balcony of the Military Club was no longer occupied, the enthusiastic crowd refused to depart and the streets still resounded with "Vive Joffre!" "Vive Pershing!" Pleased General Pershing must have been by the wild demonstration of the affection and hope, and yet he must also

179

have been made intensely serious by the appeal of two great peoples to lead them to a victory that should forever put an end to the savagery and the cruelty which the German nation, wherever it touched the world through its army, was manifesting as the controlling motive in its life.

CHAPTER XIV

A WREATH FOR THE TOMB OF LAFAYETTE

THE official calls and the ceremonies that were designed both to recognize formally the full meaning of the entrance of the United States into the world war and to arouse a fresh enthusiasm in the French people were almost at an end. General Pershing announced that on the following day he intended to begin the work for which he had come. Already the headquarters of the American Army had been established at the Rue de Constantin and the work there was in full operation.

However, there were two other visits which the American commander desired to make while he was in Paris. In Picpus Cemetery, Paris, was the tomb of Lafayette. The friendship of the young marquis, his enthusiasm for

181

the ideals of democracy and the aid he had given the colonies in America in their struggles for independence nearly a century and a half before this time, had made his name as familiar as it was beloved in the United States. He had been the personal friend of Washington, his visit to America after the new nation had been formed, his gifts and his example alike had added to the esteem in which he was held there. As Lafayette had come from France to help America so now Pershing had come from America to help France. What could be more fitting than for the American commander to manifest publicly the memories of the deep appreciation which clustered about the name of Lafayette?

Accordingly General Pershing and a half-dozen of his officers were taken to the tomb in Picpus Cemetery. There the little party was met by the Marquis and the Count de Chambrun who are direct descendants of Lafayette. Two orderlies carried a wreath of American Beauty roses which was to be placed on the tomb of the ardent young Frenchman. There were no formal or public services—the occasion being more like a token of the personal feelings of the representative of one great nation for the honored dead who had been the representative of another. The oft quoted remark of General Pershing, "Lafayette, we are here," added to the impressiveness.

General Pershing was welcomed at the cemetery quietly by the two descendants of Lafayette and by them was conducted to the tomb. The General and his fellow officers stood at salute while the orderlies were placing the wreath of roses on the marble slab that marked the final resting place of the brave and brilliant young French soldier.

In spite of the simplicity of the beautiful ceremony, however, the enthusiastic people of Paris felt that somehow they must express their appreciation of the tender and dignified tribute to one of their honored dead. Great throngs lined the streets through which the party passed, while a vast concourse assembled in the vicinity of Picpus Cemetery. Their quickly aroused sentiments had been deeply stirred. A glimpse of the passing American General was sufficient to deepen this appeal and the cheers that greeted the Americans were fervent and heartfelt.

The third day was to be the last of the formal ceremonies. General Pershing paid the formal and official calls expected of him, had luncheon with Marshal Joffre and then visited the French Senate. As soon as he and Ambassador Sharp were discovered in the diplomatic box, every senator sprang to his feet and the cheering was loud and long—"Vive l'Amerique!" "Vive l'Pershing!" It almost seemed as if the dignified senators were determined to make their salvos louder and more genuinely enthusiastic than any that had yet been heard by the distinguished visitor. Again and again General Pershing bowed in acknowledgment of his generous reception.

At last when the senators once more took their seats, Premier Ribot referred to the presence of the soldier from the United States and called upon M. Viviani to speak in acknowledgment of the event. Eloquent as

Viviani is known to be, it is said that never had his words been more expressive or appealing than on this momentous occasion. Repeatedly he was compelled to pause and wait for the applause to cease before he was able to continue his address. In his final words he referred to his own recent visit to the United States and in vivid phrases pictured the conditions as he had found them there. The ideals of civilization, the rights of free peoples, the heritage received from sires who had dearly paid for that which they bequeathed their children were to be defended and upheld. Savagery, brutality, disregard for national and individual rights were to be overthrown. Because of the ideals under which the United States had been reared and the freedom the nation had enjoyed the people were determined to share in the battle for the same privileges to be enjoyed by all mankind.

The response of the audience was instantaneous. Leaping to their feet they shouted, "Vivent les Etats Unis!" "Vive l'Amerique!" "Vive l'Pershing!" Not until after

General Pershing once more arose and again and again bowed in acknowledgment of the soul stirring tribute to him, and through him to the nation of which he was a part, was quiet restored. Even then the Senate unanimously voted a recess of a half-hour to permit the Senators personally to meet and greet the American Commander. Antonin Dubost, President of the Senate, escorted General Pershing through the imposing lobby of the Luxembourg and introduced him to the members of the Senate, one by one. The occasion served as a fitting climax to three such days as General Pershing never before had seen and the world never had known.

Of Pershing's coming to France and of his gracious, quiet manner of receiving the welcome of Paris, and his dignity that fitted every occasion, the Paris newspapers, made much. The outstanding quality, however, appeared to be his simplicity. Georges Clemenceau wrote the following tribute when the three days of welcome passed:

"Paris has given its final welcome to General

Pershing. We are justified in hoping that the acclamations of our fellow-citizens, with whom are mingled crowds of soldiers on leave, have shown him clearly right at the start in what spirit we are waging this bloodiest of wars: with what invincible determination never to falter in any fiber of our nerves or muscles.

"What does France stand for to-day but the most striking proof of the perseverance of the French spirit? I can even say that never was such a prolongation of such terrible sacrifices demanded from our people and never was it so simply and so easily obtained.

"Unless I misjudge America, General Pershing, fully conscious of the importance of his mission, has received from the cordial and joyous enthusiasm of the Parisians that kind of fraternal encouragement, which is never superfluous, even when one needs it not. Let him have no doubt that he, too, has brought encouragement to us, the whole of France that followed with its eyes his passage along the boulevards, all our hearts, that salute his coming in joy at the supreme grandeur of America's might enrolled under the standard of right. This idea M. Viviani, just back from America, splendidly developed in his eloquent speech to the Chamber in the presence of General Pershing.

"General Pershing himself, less dramatic, has given us in three phrases devoid of artificiality an impression of exceptionally virile force. It was no rhetoric, but the pure simplicity of the soldier who is here to act and who fears to promise more than he will perform. No bad sign this for those of us who have grown weary of pompous words, when we must pay so dearly for each failure of performance.

"Not long ago the Germans laughed at 'the contemptible English army' and we hear now that they regard the American army as too ridiculous for words. Well, the British have taught even Hindenburg himself what virile force can do toward filling gaps in organization. Now the arrival of Pershing brings Hindenburg news that the Americans are setting to work in their turn—those Americans whose performance in the war of secession showed them capable of such 'improvisation' of war as the world has never seen—and I think the Kaiser must be beginning to wonder whether he has not trusted rather blindly in his 'German tribal god.' He has loosed the lion from its cage, and now finds that the lion has teeth and claws to rend him.

"The Kaiser had given us but a few weeks in which to realize that the success of his submarine campaign would impose the silence of terror on the human conscience throughout the world. Well, painful as he must find it, Pershing's arrival in Paris, with its consequent military action, cannot fail to prove to him that, after all, the moral forces he ignored must always be taken into consideration in forecasting human probabilities. Those learned Boches have yet to understand that in the course of his intellectual evolution man has achieved the setting of moral right above brute force; that might is taking its stand beside right to accomplish the greatest revolution in the history of mankind.

"That is the lesson Pershing's coming has taught us, and that is why we rejoice."

Another graceful tribute was that of Maurice de Waleffe who wrote:

" 'There is no longer any Pyrenees,' said Louis XIV when he married a Spanish princess. 'There is no longer an ocean,' Pershing might say with greater justice as he is about to mingle with ours the democratic blood of his soldiers. The fusion of Europe and America is the enormous fact to note. Henceforth there is but one human race, in the Old World as in the New, and we can repeat the words of Goethe at the battle of Valmy: 'From to-day a new order of things begins.' "

In the evening after his first day of work, at the opera the enthusiasm of Paris found one more outlet for its admiration of the American General whose physical strength and bearing, whose poise and kindly appreciation of his welcome again found expression. The General arrived at the close of the first act. It was now the turn for the society of Paris to express itself. The wildest enthusiasm instantly seized upon the audience as soon as his arrival became known. As he entered his box, which was draped with the American colors, the orchestra quickly struck up the national anthem, for the moment drowning even the wild cheering of the crowded house. The curtain rose and Mme. Richardson, holding aloft a large American flag as she advanced to the front of the stage, began in English to sing the Star Spangled Banner. After each stanza the wild cheering seemed to increase in volume and enthusiasm. Then Mlle. Marthe Chenal followed and began to sing La Marseillaise. It was now the turn of the American officers and soldiers present to cheer for France; and cheer they did. A chorus of soldiers and sailors accompanied each singer. When General Pershing departed from the opera house the throngs assembled on the streets joined in another outburst. By this time even the slowest of Americans must have been fully aware that the French were glad that the commander of the Army of the United States was in Paris.

The new problem confronting the American

General was stupendous. His recommendations were to be final at Washington. In his duties he was to have the assistance of Marshal Joffre, whose ability as a soldier and whose position as the official representative of France would mean much to General Pershing. The British War Office (May 28, 1917) had said that including those already serving in French or British armies there shortly would be 100,000 American soldiers on French soil. Within a year the number was to exceed 1,000,000 and hundreds of thousands more were to follow. No such numbers or speed in transporting troops 3,500 miles had ever been known before. And in France plans must be formed, organizations made, great buildings must be erected, military measures must be adopted—and General John Joseph Pershing must be the directing power. What a task! Small cause for surprise is it that he solemnly said to a prominent clergyman before his departure from America that he "felt the need of all the help that could be given him,—human and divine."

Already in France Americans were drilling in preparation for active fighting. Among these were detachments of college students from Harvard, Princeton, Yale, University of Chicago, Williams, University of California, and many other American colleges, but a vast concourse of men from every class and condition in life in the United States was making ready to join their fellow soldiers across the sea. From no man in all the world was more expected than from General Pershing. And the expectations were resting on strong foundations if the manner in which he carried himself in the four trying days in London and in the three days of formal ceremonies in France and then in the beginnings of his heavy labors in preparing for the demands of Americans who were yet to come, were indications. By many he was declared to be the personification of the best type West Point could produce.

CHAPTER XV

THE manifestation of the feeling of France
and England for the United States as shown
to General Pershing was still further in evidence when the national holiday of each nation was celebrated. In this celebration all
three nations united. "Never did I expect to
see a day like the Fourth of July this year in
London," wrote an American stopping in that
city. "The flag of the United States was
everywhere in evidence. I don't think Great
Britain ever saw so many American flags at
one time. The streets almost seemed to be
lined with them. They were hanging from
windows, stretched across the streets and side-
walks, carried in the hands of the passing

people and everywhere were in evidence. Bands were playing the Star Spangled Banner, public meetings were held, addresses were made and dinners given—all showing that the new feeling between the countries was not only friendly but also most intensely cordial. From the King and Queen to the humblest newsboy the enthusiasm was everywhere to be seen." And what was true in London was true also throughout the kingdom.

From the front General Pershing received the following telegram:

"Dear Gen. Pershing: In behalf of myself and the whole army in France and Flanders I beg you to accept for yourself and the troops of your command my warmest greetings on American Independence Day.

"Fourth of July this year soldiers of America, France and Great Britain will spend side by side for the first time in history in defense of the great principle of liberty, which is the proudest inheritance and the most cherished possession of their several nations.

"That liberty which the British, Americans and French won for themselves they will not fail to hold not only for themselves but for the world. With the heartiest good wishes for you and your gallant army,

"Yours very sincerely,

"D. HAIG,

"Field Marshal."

To this hearty message of congratulation and good will General Pershing sent the following response to the Commander in Chief of the British Army in France and Flanders:

"MY DEAR SIR DOUGLAS: Independence Day greetings from the British armies in France, extended by its distinguished Commander in Chief, are most deeply appreciated by all ranks of the American forces. The firm unity of purpose that on the Fourth of July this year so strongly binds the great allied nations together stands as a new declaration and a new guarantee that the sacred principles of liberty shall not perish but shall be extended to all peoples.

"With the most earnest good wishes from myself and entire command to you and our brave British brothers in arms, I remain, always in great respect and high esteem,

"Yours very sincerely,

"JOHN J. PERSHING."

In Paris also the celebration was an evidence of the same or even greater enthusiasm.

Flags, bands, cheers, songs, public meetings and addresses—these all were like a repetition of the scenes that had greeted the arrival of the American commander on the soil of France. Once more General Pershing was the idol of the day, because in this way the French people best believed they could express their deep appreciation of the part America was promptly taking in the fight for freedom.

The response of America was equally strong when ten days later the great country, more than 3,000 miles away, joined in a hearty celebration of the French national holiday—Bastile Day. As Lafayette had brought to and presented to the United States the key to the famous old prison so it seemed almost as if the key had unlocked the doors of every American heart. The French flag was flying from thousands of buildings. The French national air was heard on every side.

In America, too, just as there had been a brief time before in France, there were great assemblies quickly aroused to the highest pitch of enthusiasm by the words of orators describing the marvelous heroism and devotion of France in the present world war. As one famous speaker said, "France had not only found her soul and surprised the world by her devotion; she had even surprised herself."

Perhaps the celebration in America reached its highest point in a vast meeting in the Madison Square Garden in New York City on the evening of July 14th. One newspaper glowingly described the vast concourse that filled the Garden: "It isn't too much to say that perhaps the air quivered no more violently around the Bastile on that great day in Paris 129 years ago, than it did in Madison Square Garden last night when at the apex of a day of glorious tribute to France a tall young man wearing the horizon blue of the French army and noted throughout the world for his singing, sang with splendid fervor France's— and now in a way our own—'La Marseillaise.'

The Garden fairly rocked with the applause, as banners and flags were waved in the hands of the excited, shouting throng. French soldiers with the little marks upon their sleeves that showed the bravery on the battlefield of the men privileged to wear them, soldiers and sailors of many lands, war-nurses in their cool white costumes, men who had fought in France, Belgium, Serbia, Italy, at Gallipoli, at the Marne and at Verdun—and many more were there to assist in expressing the feelings of America for her ally.

"They shall not pass"—it was almost like the determination of the men that doggedly stood before and blocked the Germans as they did their utmost to drive through Verdun.

A message from General Foch was read by the chairman, Charles E. Hughes. "After four years of struggle the plans of the enemy for domination are stopped," began Judge Hughes, but he also was compelled to "stop" until the deafening applause that interrupted the reading of the message from the great French commander had quieted down sufficiently to enable him to proceed. After several minutes passed he resumed. "He (the enemy) sees the numbers of his adversaries increase each day and the young American army bring into the battle a valor and a faith without equal; is not this a sure pledge of the definite triumph of the just cause?"

If the true answer to the question of the commander of all the armies of the allies was to be measured by the mighty roar that spontaneously arose, then the General must have been convinced as well as satisfied.

"We are doing more to-night than paying tribute," declared the chairman. "We are here to make our pledge. We make our pledge to the people of France. We make our pledge and it is the pledge of a people able to redeem it."

Secretary of the Navy Daniels read a message from President Wilson: "America greets France on this day of stirring memories, with a heart full of warm friendship and of devotion to the great cause in which the two peoples are now so happily united. July 14th, like our own July 4th, has taken on a new significance not only for France but for the world. As France celebrated our Fourth of July, so do we celebrate her Fourteenth, keenly conscious

199

of a comradeship of arms and of purpose of which we are deeply proud.

"The sea seems very narrow to-day, France is a neighbor to our hearts. The war is being fought to save ourselves from intolerable things, but it is also being fought to save mankind. We extend our hands to each other, to the great peoples with whom we are associated and the peoples everywhere who love right and prize justice as a thing beyond price, and consecrate ourselves once more to the noble enterprise of peace and justice, realizing the great conceptions that have lifted France and America high among the free peoples of the earth.

"The French flag floats to-day from the staff of the White House and America is happy to do honor to that flag."

A similar statement was made by Great Britain's ambassador, the Earl of Reading, who declared that Bastile Day was also being celebrated throughout the British Empire.

The climax came when Ambassador Jusserand spoke:

"Your national fete and ours have the same meaning: Emancipation. The ideal they represent is so truly the same, that it is no wonder, among the inspiring events in which we live, that France celebrated the other day your Fourth and you are now celebrating our Fourteenth. We owe so much to each other in our progress toward Freedom.

"Those enthusiastic French youths who served under Washington, Rochambeau and Lafayette had seen liberty and equality put into practice, and had brought back to France the seed, which sown at an opportune moment, sprang up and grew wonderfully.

"The two greatest events in our histories are closely connected. Between the end of your revolution and the beginning of ours, there elapsed only six years. Our flag, devised the day after the fall of the Bastile, combining the same colors as your own, is just a little younger than your Old Glory, born in revolutionary times. And the two, floating for the first time together over the trenches of distant France, defying the barbaric enemy, have much to say to each other, much about the past, much about the future.

"United as we are with the same firmness of purpose, we shall advance our standards and cause the enemy to understand that the best policy is honesty, respect of others' freedom and respect of the sworn pledge.

"That song of freedom, the 'Marseillaise' will

again be sung at the place of its birth, that Alsatian song born in Strassburg, justifying its original title, a 'War song of the Rhine.'

"The place where he shall stop is not, however, written on the map, but in our hearts, a kind of map the enemy has been unable to decipher. But what is written is plain enough, and President Wilson is even plainer in his memorable speech at the Tomb of Washington on your own Fourth. It comes to this: 'One more Bastile remains to be taken, representing feudalism, autocracy, despotism, the German one, and when it falls, peace will reign again.' "

And over in France was an American— brave, kind of heart, dignified and tremendously in earnest who stood before the people of the old world as the very personification of the spirit that animated the new world.

CHAPTER XVI

INCIDENTS AND CHARACTERISTICS

ONE of the most striking elements in the grip which General Pershing has upon his soldiers is well shown by the following extract from a letter which a quiet, unknown doughboy recently sent from France to his mother: "I think I forgot to tell you that Pershing looked us over. He is a wonderful man to look at. Power is written all over his face. Believe me, with a man like that in the lead we ought to win, hands down. Just one look commands respect and confidence."

One reason for this confidence doubtless is the frequently expressed opinion which the commander also has of his men. Again and again he has publicly declared that the idealism of the American soldier boys was bound to win this war. "They will defend these ideals

203

at any sacrifice.'' And those who are aware of the spirit of many a young American student in college or worker on some quiet farm, will understand why General Pershing has made so much of this idealism which he says is the backbone of the American fighting men in France.

It is not only the General, but the man Pershing behind the General that makes its appeal and finds its response from the American boys. In every Y. M. C. A. hut in France to-day there is hanging a picture of the leader of the American armies. Underneath this picture are the following words, which bear his own signature:

''Hardship will be your lot but trust in God will give you comfort. Temptation will befall you but the teaching of our Saviour will give you strength. Let your valor as a soldier and your conduct as a man be an inspiration to your comrades and an honor to your country.''

The meaning of these words perhaps becomes more apparent if for a moment they are placed in contrast with the reported relations existing between the German soldiers and their officers, sometimes driven into battle by brutal methods, threatened, kicked and beaten, and if they protested, sometimes the gunners were chained to their guns—small cause for surprise is it that the American boys fail to appreciate the "blessings" of autocracy or are determined that the brutality and aims of all war lords shall forever perish from the earth.

Then, too, his personal interest in the young American fighter who has done something to deserve recognition is one of his elements of strength. There must, however, first have been given an indication that the deed was worthy of praise—for General Pershing's commendation is not cheap nor does he scatter it promiscuously. The following incident may be looked upon as typical

John Kulolski, born in Poland, emigrant to the United States, enlisted at Buffalo, New York, June 7, 1916. In the following year, on his birthday, he reënlisted and on the same month and day in 1918 he was sent to the trenches. Indeed, he declared that his birthday "always brought something great into his life." His first service in the army was as a cook, but at his own request he was transferred to the fighting forces. Cooking might be necessary, but it was "too slow for him." Soon in the Bois de Belleau he found his opportunity. The fighting was savage and John Kulolski's company was in peril from a nearby gunners' nest. Suddenly, without orders and with the new spirit of initiative which had been acquired by the young Pole in America, he darted ahead alone, and by the sheer force of his own impetuous act charged the gun and made prisoners of the gun crew and its officer. Doubtless his very daring caused his enemies to believe that he was not alone but was one of many who were about to attack them. At all events the Germans surrendered to John Kulolski and his bravery was quickly known all along the line.

To him as soon as he heard of his daring deed General Pershing sent the following telegram from headquarters:

"For Private Kulolski, Company (deleted).

"I have just heard of your splendid conduct on

June 6th when you alone charged a gun, captured it and its crew, together with an officer. I have awarded you the Distinguished Service Cross. I congratulate you.

"PERSHING."

Who does not know that Kulolski's deed and the commander's quick and personal as well as official recognition of the heroism of this private soldier at once aroused a spirit of gratitude and enthusiasm not only in the heart of the young Pole, but also caused a thrill in the heart of every doughboy in the ranks that heard the story?

From Paris, July 22, 1918, the Associated Press sent the following despatch:

"Your country is proud of you, and I am more than proud to command such men as you. You have fought splendidly."

General Pershing thus addressed wounded American soldiers lying in the American Red Cross hospitals in Paris to-day. In each ward of every hospital he talked to the men. He inquired if they were being well cared for, how and where they were wounded, what regiments they belonged to, and expressed his sympathy to scores of patients.

General Pershing also talked to the physicians, surgeons, and nurses, and thanked them for the work they were doing in caring for the wounded.

"No one can ask of any fighting force more than that they should do as well as you have done," he said to his troops. The General added that he wished he could speak personally with each and every man in the hospital, but this was impossible. So he asked Major James H. Perkins to repeat his message and say to each individual man, "The American people are proud of you."

It is a very devoted and democratic army which General Pershing commands in France. Those who know him personally have a deep affection for him for they understand what he is. Those who do not have a personal acquaintance admire him no less for what they believe him to be. It is a common remark in the ranks, even by those who never even saw their leader, "What a fine man Pershing is." His nickname

"Black Jack" is an expression of admiration and affection, as much so as when the French poilus tenderly refer to "Papa" Joffre.

Whenever General Pershing in his scattered duties arrives at a place where there are wounded American soldiers he never fails to find a few brief minutes when he can visit these boys and speak a word of affectionate appreciation of what they have done. It is usually, however, not to his own but to his country's pride and sympathy that he refers. "Your country is proud of you." Sometimes it is just a handclasp, sometimes only a glance from his dark eyes, expressive of the deep interest and pride in his soldier boys that he can give the wounded. He is a man of few words and as a consequence every spoken word counts.

A direct report states that "faces are brighter, eyes have a new expression whenever, which is as often as the crush of his duties permits—he visits a hospital."

One further incident will illustrate the many-sided activities of the American General. One evening at a certain nameless point he found that he had a very few minutes free before his automobile was to rush him to the next place he was to visit. Instantly he decided to visit the Y. M. C. A. hut. As he drew near he found that a couple of hundred boys were in the building and that someone was "banging the piano" with a furious rag-time. Hobnailed shoes were noisily keeping time to the music and the lusty voices of the shouting and singing young soldiers were plainly heard far beyond the building. Not one of the boys was aware that the commander was anywhere in the vicinity.

Suddenly a yell arose near the entrance. Instantly every soldier turned to discover the cause of the break. "General Pershing" ran as a loud whisper throughout the assembly and instantly every one of the assembled doughboys sprang to his feet and stood at attention. Then no longer able to repress or restrain their feelings they united in such an enthusiastic yell as might have revealed their presence to an enemy if he was not too far away.

Quickly the General was in the midst of the

throng and was telling his admirers just how he had "dropped in to see how they were getting along." He was delighted, he told them, to find everything in good order and expressed his deep satisfaction with the manner in which they were doing their part in the gigantic struggle. "Your country is proud of you."

Small cause for wonder is it that it is currently reported that "no army ever went to the battlefield better protected against the pitfalls of army life than the American forces in France." Every friendly and helpful activity receives his cordial support—Red Cross, Y. M. C. A., Knights of Columbus, Salvation Army and all. He is deeply concerned not only with the quality and quantity of the work in France but also with the reports that are to go back home concerning what the boys are doing on the far distant fields of France. Still more is he concerned about the effects of their stay upon the boys themselves. "Everything possible is being done to see that these young Americans who will return home some day shall go back clean."

He is deeply interested in all the athletics and sports of his troops. He simply is insistent upon one main quality, "everything must be clean."

A certain reporter for a New York newspaper sends the following incident:

Passing a dark corner one night I encountered a M. P. (Military Policeman). Some of the M. P.s are a bit rough. They have to be, and they would wade into a den of wildcats.

"Hey, you pencil pusher," he called, "did you see the big boss?"

I had.

"Well," he said, "you've flashed your lamps on the finest man that ever stood in shoe leather."

One day General Pershing arrived at a station where a motley crowd greeted his coming. The following day there was posted on a bulletin board of the barracks a cordial commendation of the young French officer who had so efficiently done his duty at the station in handling the somewhat unruly assembly at the arrival of the American commander and his staff. That is General Pershing's way. Quietly cordial, looking for good in every one of his men and usually finding it, a strict disciplinarian and quick to punish neglect or an evil deed, he is the idol of the army.

"General Pershing is one of the finest men I ever met. Everybody in the army admires him greatly," declares a prominent American officer, and another adds, "I have never met a nobler man in my life than General Pershing."

According to a statement of an orderly sergeant of the commander, the General has a regular order for beginning the work of every day. Rising at five o'clock there is first a half hour of setting up exercises which the two men take together. Next the General, although he is at an age when most men abandon running except as a necessity or a last resort, goes out for a run of fifteen minutes. Later there is a united attack upon the medicine ball and there is no slight or "ladylike" exercise. Although the sergeant is twenty-five years younger than the General, he acknowledges that he is usually the first to declare that he has had sufficient for the beginning of the day.

The hour of retirement is usually eleven o'clock, and just before that time there are more setting up exercises, after which the sergeant says he himself is entirely reconciled to the suggestion to turn in.

In this way and because he has followed this somewhat strenuous plan since he was a young man General Pershing has kept himself in magnificent physical condition.

Indeed, the sergeant said that in the ten years during which he had been the commander's orderly he has never known but one day when the General was incapicitated for his duties. That day was in the early rush of the punitive expedition into Mexico to get Villa. The change of water or perhaps the quality of it made him ill, but even then, in spite of the surgeon's advice for him to remain quietly in his tent for a day or two, General Pershing, unmindful of the influence of his example, "disobeyed orders" and resumed his work. Fortunately no ill effects followed his disobedience.

A tender touch in the sergeant's statement is one upon which we have no right to enlarge though the fact is as suggestive as it is characteristic. The first duty of the orderly in unpacking the General's belongings when they move to new quarters is to take the photograph of Mrs. Pershing and the four children as the family was before that terrible fire in the Presidio, and place it in a desk or bureau where it is easily seen. Often the General sits in silence before it, and as he looks at the family group, the sergeant believes that, for the time, the tragedy is forgotten and to the silent soldier his family again seems to be complete. It is an occasion into which an outsider, however, has no right to enter and however strong may be his sympathy, the sorrow is too intensely personal for even a close friend to obtrude.

In the letter which General Pershing wrote from Mindanao to his classmates on the occasion of their twenty-fifth anniversary of their graduation from West Point he lightly referred to his difficulties in acquiring French. In view of his ancestry, for his name and lineage can be traced back to Alsace, this at first may appear somewhat strange; but the statement is his own. However, when he first went to France his fluency in the language of the people of that country was not sufficient to satisfy him and an interpreter was provided, who usually was present when he met with French officers who were as ignorant of his language as he was of theirs. In a brief time, however, the interpreter was discarded. General Pershing, in spite of the difficulty of acquiring a new language when one is older, was soon conversing in their own tongue with Marshal Joffre, General Petain and General Foch. Just what the opinion of his accent was we do not know and they doubtless were too polite to express it. The essential point, however, is that just as the American Commander years before had learned the language of the Moros in order to assist him in his task of dealing with the little brown people, so he resolutely set to work to learn French, at least to an extent that enabled him to understand what was said in his presence and to express himself to his friends without the aid of an interpreter.

Not long before the raid upon Columbus by

Villa and his bandits General Pershing, in a letter from which the following extract is taken, wrote: "We do not want war if we can honestly avoid it, but we must not hesitate to make war if the cause of civilization and progress demands it. Nearly every step in human progress has been at the sacrifice of human life. There are some things dearer even than life. If a nation has set up high ideals either for itself or for others it must be prepared to enforce those ideals if need be by armies and navies. Of course it would be better to enforce them through moral prestige." These sentiments were expressed long before the declaration of war with Germany or the President had written his famous words about making the world safe for democracy. They are doubly interesting for that reason and expressive of General Pershing's innermost feelings when there was every reason why he should express himself freely. Most brilliant American fighters have not been lovers of war for its own sake. Washington was reluctant to enter upon war, although when he believed there was no escape he fought to the uttermost limit of his power. General Grant's most frequently quoted words are not warlike, but "Let us have peace." And General Pershing is not one whit behind the other two.

Early in July, 1918, Chairman Hurley sent a cablegram to the American fighting men in France that the shipbuilders at home would launch one hundred merchant ships July 4th. Promptly from General Pershing came the following appreciative and defiant acknowledgment: "The launching of one hundred ships on the Fourth of July is the most inspiring news that has come to us. All ranks of the Army in France send their congratulations and heartfelt thanks to their patriotic brothers in the shipyards at home. No more defiant answer could be given to the enemy's challenge. With such backing we cannot fail to win. All hail American shipbuilders."

His quick sense of appreciation is seen also in the following telegram which he sent Premier Clemenceau after the hearty congratulations sent by the great Frenchman on the occa-

sion of the parade of American troops in Paris
in the celebration of the Fourth of July:

"Permit me to tell you how much I am touched
by the cordial telegram you sent me. I shall not
fail to make it known to the troops in question. All
the officers and men of the troops who had the privi-
lege of participating in the Fourth of July ceremony
in Paris will retain unforgettable recollections of
the enthusiastic reception accorded to them. Proud
of the confidence France places in them they are
heartened more than ever to do their duty until
common victory comes."

One day in France he saw two American
soldiers at work on a woodpile. One glance was
sufficient to show him that the two men were
working out a form of punishment for some
misdeed. As we know General Pershing is a
believer in strict and if necessary stern discipline. Soon after coming to France he had
ordered one American soldier to be hanged for
a nameless crime and several others to be disciplined severely for drunkenness. Believing in
the best and hoping and expecting the good in
every one of his men to manifest itself, never-

theless he is severe when severity is demanded. And he was at once interested when he first saw the two American boys at the wood pile, manifestly serving a sentence of some kind.

Stopping his automobile, General Pershing sent his orderly to find out what the offense was for which the two soldiers were serving their sentence. Upon the orderly's return he reported that the two men had taken "French leave" of their company several days before this time. They were jealous because certain of their fellows "had been sent up ahead to fight" while they had been left behind. And they were eager to fight. They had enlisted and come to France for that express purpose. And now to be left behind! The thought was more than the two Yankee boys could endure. Fight they could and fight they would—with or without specific orders from their officers. And fight they did, for without any ceremony they departed for the front one night and kept on going until they found it. According to their own story they "found war and mixed in." And also they were found out and sentenced to serve five days at the woodpile as a penalty for their disobedience and over-hasty zeal. It is said General Pershing hastily departed from the spot and that he laughed heartily at the story of Americans who were punished not because they were not willing to fight, but were so eager that they did not wait for such a little thing as orders or commands. And then the General fell to talking about his favorite theme—the daring and bravery of his men in the campaign against the Moros.

One day in Paris, General Pershing saw a tiny man—a dwarf—upon the sidewalk of the street through which he was passing at the time. The little man instantly recalled to the commander the wedding of Datto Dicky of Jolo. The little chieftain was about to be married. There was a current report that he was the smallest man in the world, but the statement has not been verified. At all events, whatever he may have lacked in stature he more than made up in his power over the tribe of which he was a chief.

At a fair in Zamboanga, Datto Dicky was

about to take unto himself a wife, the little lady being as diminutive as her prospective husband. After the formal wedding General Pershing presented to the bride a tiny house in every way adapted to the needs of such a diminutive couple. The dwelling stood on stilts on the beach, a thing of beauty in the eyes of all the Moros that were attending the fair.

The tiny chieftain and his bride gratefully accepted the present of the little building, which they occupied during their honeymoon. Upon their return to Jolo they in turn gave their present to the children of the General and they used it as a playhouse. As Datto Dicky is said to have been just two feet and three inches in height the little children of the American governor doubtless found the structure much to their liking and well adapted to their needs. They were as delighted over Dicky's generosity to them as the diminutive chieftain had been over the unexpected gift their father had given him.

The following incidents are taken from the New York *Times:*

"About ten years ago he and Mrs. Pershing were in Paris and the General, who was then a captain, was suffering from a slight indisposition, which his doctor thought might be attributable to smoking. Upon Mrs. Pershing's insistence the captain went to Mannheim where there was a famous cure. The resident doctor examined him and advised that he give up smoking. It happened that Pershing had always been an inveterate smoker. His cigar was a part of his life. He wrestled with the question a day or two and made up his mind that he would follow the medical advice.

"When asked if he hadn't found the job a hard one and whether he wasn't still tempted the reply was:

"'Not in the least, the only hard thing was in making up his mind. He had hardly given the matter a thought since.'

"There are two subjects which the General will always talk about with interest—his farming experience and his four years with the Moros in the Philippines.

"He loves to hark back to those days when his highest obligation was to get out into the cornfield at the very earliest minute in the morning that there was daylight enough to see the ears of corn. When he was fourteen he took the management of the farm. His father had been a rich man, but the panic of 1873 broke him. John was the oldest of nine children and he had to go to the front. In everything that he does now I can detect the influence of his early training. I can see in the General of to-day the farmer boy with his contempt of hardship, the country school teacher with his shepherding instinct for those around him and the general wariness of country bringing-up. It is inexorably true that the boy is father to the man."

CHAPTER XVII

WHAT OTHERS THINK OF HIM

IN quoting a few words from the opinions others have expressed concerning the American Commander doubtless some of them may seem to be a trifle too laudatory. It is not to be forgotten that the words of those who perhaps did not fully share the sentiments have not been recorded. If such opinions exist, their record has not been brought to·the attention of the writer. As a rule, Americans have no comparative degree in their estimates of men. They like a man or they do not like him. He is either a success or a failure, good or bad, wise or foolish. Between the two extremes there is little standing room, and into one catagory or the other they cast nearly everyone. If General Pershing has not escaped this condition, his consolation doubtless is that he is merely sharing the common lot of his fellow-citizens.

A close friend has this to say of him: "You should meet him at a dinner party and listen to his stories. You should stand with him before his tent in the field, in the sunshine—he loves the sunshine and the wide out-of-doors—and hear him tell stories of his campaigning at his best. You should meet this big man with the heart of a little child, this man who by befriending his enemies has made them his companions, this man who stands up erect and faces the horrors of disaster with a smile and prays in his heart for the sufferers."

Another friend says: "There is something about Pershing that reminds one of Lincoln. It may be his ready wit and never failing good humor or perhaps his big sympathetic heart. In the army the similarity is frequently pointed out."

An officer who served under him in the Punitive Expedition into Mexico and was thrown into close relations with him writes: "I have had the pleasure of knowing many of our

226

great men, but Pershing is the biggest of them all. He combines the rugged simplicity of Lincoln with the dogged perseverance of Grant; the strategic mystical ability of Stonewall Jackson and the debonair personality of McClellan. In one quality, that of intuition, he may be inferior possibly to Roosevelt, but in cold logic and in supreme knowledge of human nature and of soldier nature I have never met his equal."

The colonel of his regiment when Pershing was a lieutenant in the 10th Cavalry said of him: "I have been in many fights but on my word he is the bravest and coolest man under fire I ever saw."

In 1903, Elihu Root, then Secretary of State, in President McKinley's cabinet, cabled him: "The thanks of the War Department for the able and effective accomplishment of a difficult and important task."

A simpler, but no less effective estimate of his character, although it was given in a way to puzzle him and perhaps also was a source of embarrassment was the act of the Sultan of Oato who officially made young Major Pershing the "father" of his eighteen-year-old boy. This was the highest tribute the ruler of the tribe could pay, to give his own son to the American officer. And this was done, too, when by his training and religion the Mohammedan chieftain looked down upon even if he did not despise a Christian.

Georges Clemenceau, whose words have been previously quoted, has this to say concerning the directness and simplicity of the American General: "General Pershing has given us in three phrases devoid of artificiality, an impression of exceptionally virile force. It was no rhetoric, but pure simplicity of the soldier who is here to act and who fears to promise more than he will perform. No bad sign this, for those of us who have grown weary of pompous words when we must pay dearly for each failure of performance."

An intimate friend of his boyhood writes: "John was and still is intensely human and that is why we all love him. His old playmates and friends are proud of his success as a soldier, but they love him because of his high standard of principles and unswerving integrity. John J. Pershing is revered by the entire population of Linn County, Missouri, and I hope in the near future to see a statue of Pershing erected in the beautiful town park of Laclede, in his honor.''

A well-known college president writes of him: ''It is his foresight as distinct from vision which has most impressed me. He sees what ought to be done and then does it. His spirit of determination, his persistence, his foresightedness, seem to me the predominant traits in a well-rounded character. Strength rather than brilliancy, solidity, reliability, saneness are other terms by which the same qualities might be defined.''

Another distinguished president of a college in General Pershing's native State makes the following analysis: ''I have been here twenty-six years and have had a good deal to do with young men. I have never seen a man yet that had these characteristics that failed in his life work:

"*First,* Pershing's modesty.

"*Second,* His friendliness—his ability to get along with his fellows.

"*Third,* His industry.

"*Fourth,* What the boys call, 'everlastingly on the job'—always in his place, always had his lessons, always performed his duties.

"*Fifth,* His courage in facing every obstacle.

"*Sixth,* His forward look—his looking ahead.

"My secretary adds that I have omitted one of the strongest of General Pershing's attributes—his sense of right."

It is a great asset when the people of a man's native town speak of him, even of his boyhood, in terms of affection and confidence. It is to his credit when school and college mates write of their belief in his sterling character. It is a source of pride when the early efforts of a young man, in the trying days of his first experiences in his chosen profession, find a cordial response to his efforts and it is a still deeper source of gratification when he has done his best and has received recognition and reward from the nation at large. And then when maturer days have came and the glitter and the glamour have lost much of their appeal, for one to find that the great ones of the earth recognize and value more highly than the doer the deeds he has done—all this is a heritage the children and the coming generations will receive with grateful hearts. All these are a part of the possessions of General John Joseph Pershing.

The supreme honor thus far which General Pershing has received is the recognition from his own country which found its expression in his appointment as General, October 6, 1917, "with rank from that date, during the existence of the present emergency, under the provisions of an Act of Congress approved October 6, 1917."

When, on October 8, 1917, he accepted this appointment what thoughts must have been in his mind. He had then received the highest military honor the United States of America could bestow upon a soldier. He was the successor in office of Washington, Grant, Sherman and Sheridan. What a wonderful list of honored names it is! And a half-century had elapsed since anyone had received such an appointment. The wildest dream of the young captain of cadets at West Point had come true. And he had expressed his opinion just before he went to West Point that there would be slight opportunity for promotion in the permanent peace which apparently had settled over the nations of the earth. It is a source of comfort to learn that even the wisest and the best of men are sometimes compelled to revise their judgments.

It is not incredible that the gift which Marshal Joffre provided, or at least one in which he was the prime instigator, the presentation of a small gold-mounted sword for General Pershing's little son, Warren, may have touched the General's heart as deeply as any honor he ever received. A sword from the Field Marshal of France, given in the greatest war ever fought by mankind! And we may be sure that however kindly the feeling of the foremost soldiers of France may have been for little Warren Pershing the gift nevertheless was made to the boy because he is the son of his father.

A similar method of expressing the regard for the father by a gift to his son was followed in an incident in the celebration of Bastile Day in Paris, July 14, 1918. At the general headquarters of the American Army in France the members of the graduating class of the Lycee presented to the American Commander a marvelously bound volume of episodes in the history of France. This beautiful work, however, was "to be transmitted to Warren Pershing from his comrades of the Lycee."

What other people than the French would have thought of such a dainty and yet effective way of expressing their admiration of a man? Sometimes a son objects to being known chiefly because he bears the name of his father. It is seldom, however, that a man ever objects to being known as the father of his son.

Just before this volume was given by the students, General Pershing had presented their diplomas to the members of the graduating class of the Lycee. This very pleasing duty had followed after he had formally received the American troops and the French societies which had marched through the streets that were gay with brilliant decorations and thronged by cheering thousands.

On August 7, 1918, there appeared in many American newspapers the following brief and simple message from France:

"With the American Armies in France, Aug. 6.

"President Poincare personally decorated General Pershing with the Grand Cross of the Legion of Honor this morning with impressive military ceremonies at American General Headquarters."

This was all that was cabled, but a column would not have added to the meaning. As far as military recognition was concerned France could do no more. Her choicest honor, the one most highly prized by her patriotic soldiers, had been bestowed upon a soldier from across the sea, not only as a token of her esteem for the man, but also for the country which had chosen him to be the leader of her armies.

Nor was this the only honor of its kind. England already had shown her appreciation by awarding him the Grand Cross of the Order of the Bath—an honor which it is said was then bestowed for the first time upon a soldier of a foreign nation, or at least upon a soldier from the United States.* And other similar orders and decorations were given and by different nations. It is difficult in democratic America to appreciate just how much such recognition means in the lands in which they were so generously bestowed. We may be certain, however, that these honors, which are rare, were not bestowed thoughtlessly and that General Pershing was deeply appreciative in each instance of the motive and feeling that lay behind the gift.

Without question, the honor which most deeply touches the General is the confidence and affection of the men he commands. This is more and deeper than mere popularity. The latter varies and shifts as a weathercock veers

* Beyond the cabled report the writer is unable to verify this statement.

with the changing winds. Many of the world's great characters have not only not had it, but have suffered martyrdom because they or their teachings were unpopular. But the deep regard, the confidence and pride which the American forces universally manifest for their leader are based primarily, not upon their impulses or impressions, but upon their belief in the qualities he has quietly manifested, the record he has made, and the power of his own personality.

Deeply impressed as the American commander must be by the receptions given him, the formal honors bestowed upon him by his own and other countries, there is still a minor chord that sounds in the chorus of acclaim. What would the mother, who in the little Missouri village first fired his boyish heart with an earnest desire to make the most of himself, say now if she was here to treasure in her heart the words that have been spoken in memory of the deeds he has done? And his wife—if she had not perished in the fire at the Presidio, and now could follow his career with the pride which a good woman ever has in the recognition of her husband, what added strength her sympathy and fellowship would give to the arm and heart of the man whose name and lot she shared. Sometimes there are tragedies for our soldiers greater even than the battlefields provide.

CHAPTER XVIII

As a Writer and Speaker

THE two predominant qualities that have marked General Pershing in other lines of activity naturally appear in his written and spoken words. These are simplicity and forcefulness.

He writes but little and then only when he has something to say. What he has to say he tells and then stops. His style is lucid and interesting; even his early reports make good reading.

Certain of his sayings have almost the force of proverbs. For example, when one has once heard, "Germany can be beaten; Germany must be beaten; Germany will be beaten," he can never forget the terse epigrammatic phrasing. The same thing is true also of his response to the message of the French school children who invaded his headquarters, bringing their Fourth of July greetings:

> To-day constitutes a new Declaration of Independence, a solemn oath that the liberty for which France has long been fighting will be attained.

It is not much when measured in words, but it is enough when behind it is the man.

Similarly terse and appealing are his words already referred to, hanging in every Y. M. C. A. hut in France.

He is not an orator in the sense of being oratorical, but he is conversational, direct and impressive in public address. His soldierly bearing, his fine physique, clear voice and strong face are accessories of no small value.

There is a field in which General Pershing has been a pronounced success as a speaker which perhaps is not commonly known, and that is at dinners and similar public functions. Anyone who notes the corners of Pershing's mouth, at once is aware that the General possesses a keen sense of humor. No better illustration could be given of this fact than an incident not long ago recorded in the *Missouri Historical Review:*

"He was invited to a stag dinner party one evening where a jolly story-telling lot of good fellows were to be present and he went primed with his best stories, a memorandum in his vest pocket to aid him in telling them. The memorandum was accidentally dropped on the floor and was picked up by one of his friends, who immediately saw what it was and decided to have his little joke at the General's expense. The finder got an opportunity to spring the first story and promptly started off with the first one on the list. Pershing said nothing and laughed —he always does when a good story is told, and makes you laugh, too—but when the second one on his list was told he felt in his pocket for the memorandum and discovered its loss. A few minutes later the General, after a consultation with a waiter, announced that he had just received a message which would require his absence for a few minutes on important business.

"Jumping into a car he was hurried to a hotel. From the clerk he secured the names of half a dozen traveling men—drummers—who were stopping there and announced that he wanted to see these men at once on important business. The drummers responded and in twenty minutes the General was back at the banquet, before the coffee had been poured, with a new stock of yarns. Then ensued a battle

royal between the two famous raconteurs, much to
the amusements of the guests, until his friend played
out the string and left the General victor in the
humorous contest.

"Just at this juncture one of the drummers, made
up as a police officer, arrived, arrested the joker,
searched him and found the General's memorandum,
which he exposed to the hilarious guests with the
significant comment: 'General Pershing has really
been the only entertainer this evening, but lots of
people are making reputations with the public on the
General's ideas.' "

His words to the British public and his public address in France are alike notable for their
simplicity and directness, their friendliness and
dignity. He understands thoroughly his part.
It is a great advantage for America to have a
representative for whose public utterances no
apology must be made and no explanations
given.

CHAPTER XIX

The Man Behind the General

It would be as impertinent as it is impossible for one who has not been associated with General Pershing for a long time directly and closely to attempt anything like an analysis of the man or his career. There are, nevertheless, certain qualities that have become more or less the possessions of the public because they have been manifested in his public service. It is therefore permissible to refer briefly to certain of them.

As a foundation for all his work is a strong, vigorous body which at all times has been cared for in a way to make it the servant and not the master of the man. Regular and somewhat strenuous physical exercise maintains the uniformly excellent health and vigor of the Commander. Naturally strong, hard work developed his strength in his boyhood, and his military career has made many demands upon as well as increased these powers. Even when he entered West Point he was an acknowledged expert in horsemanship and his early work in the ten years of his campaigns against the Indians, certainly tested his skill to the utmost in this particular line.

He has known almost every form of active service the American Army can provide. In the demands for rough or heavy work excellent judges asserted when he was sent to France that he has no superior and since his arrival he has shown that he was equally at home in the finer and higher demands that were made upon him. His distinguished bearing, his physical vigor and good health have provided an excellent foundation. The old Latin proverb *Mens sana in corpore sano* has certainly been verified in the life of General Pershing.

It was Oliver Wendell Holmes who has been frequently quoted as having said that "the foremost qualification for success is the proper selection of one's grandparents." The forcefulness of General Pershing's father, the inspiring words of his mother form a rare background. "Foremost citizen," "devoted to his family," "sterling," "ambitious"—these are some of the words of old-time friends and neighbors, descriptive and expressive of their estimates of his father. All of them, however, are not more suggestive and tender than a neighbor's description of the General's mother as a "splendid homemaker," and "an inspiration to her children." There are many things a son cherishes more highly than the inheritance of great riches, and foremost is the heritage of a good name.

As the oldest of nine children naturally he learned and assumed certain responsibilities at an early age. With the advice and help of his mother it is said that even when he was only fourteen he was managing a farm in the absence of his father. There was work to be done and in abundance. There is ancient authority for the claim that it is good to "learn to bear the yoke in one's youth." A "yoke," however, is not the burden, it is a contrivance which enables one to bear his burden.

A prominent and successful man of business in New York City declared not long ago that if a man does not learn to work when he is young (this man placed the limit at twenty-two) he does not learn afterward. This was the result of both observation and experience.

Whether or not these conclusions are correct, certain it is that in the case of General Pershing, as it has been also in many other marked instances, he learned not only to work but also learned how to work when he was only a boy.

His birthplace was in the great state of Missouri. Reference has already been made to the semi-slang expression which indicates that a man from that State "must be shown." Not long ago there appeared in one of the foremost newspapers of America a bit of verse applying this saying to the present gigantic task of the Commander of the American Expeditionary Forces in France. The following quotation (*The Evening Telegram*), whatever it may lack in poetic flavor, is expressive of the public conception of the meaning of the statement:

"When 'Jack' Pershing left for Europe
    With his sturdy fighting men,
Kaiser Willy said, 'How silly!
    I'll annihilate them when
I have time to bother with 'em,
    For that peewee Yankee force
Won't be in it for a minute
    With my Prussian troops, of course.' "

"Is that so? Well, Kaiser Willy
    You have made a foolish bet,
You have boasted, then you've roasted,
    But you haven't whipped 'em yet.
Let this, Kaiser, make you wiser,
    If you really care to know,
Jack was born in old Missouri,
    He's a man you'll 'have to show.' "

"Pershing, Pershing, 'Black Jack' Pershing,
    We are with you, one and all,
We will ever pull the lever
    That will make the Prussians fall.
Fighting Pershing,—yes, we know you,
    Old Missouri born and bred,
Here's our motto, we will show you,
    'All together! Forge ahead!' "

His determination is one of his fundamental qualities. It is seen in the very expression of his face, emphasized by the prominent nose and jaw. Although it was doubtless a heritage, nevertheless the trying experiences of his early days intensified and aided in developing the quality.

He knew the meaning of hard work when he was a boy, as has been said, but it did not shake his ultimate purpose. He was eager to obtain an education and with this determination once fixed in his mind he never relaxed. Working, teaching, saving, when he entered the Kirksville Normal School he understood something of the price he was paying for the advantages he received. He knew what the attendance had cost him and it is easily understood why he was determined to get the worth of his money.

At West Point this same element was still prominent. It impressed his classmates and teachers. He saw what he wanted and wasted no time or effort on "asides" that might interfere. To be senior captain of cadets was to him the supreme honor—therefore it was only natural that he won the appointment.

The same spirit carried him through his campaign in the Philippine Islands. The Moros could be brought to reason, therefore the Moros were brought to reason. It animates him in France—"Germany can be beaten," "Germany must be beaten," and the third clause is as natural as the words of the General can make them —"Germany will be beaten." It is fitting that the commander of the best trained army America ever had should lead it in a spirit of determination that cannot be shaken.

Underneath this firmness is an unfailing spirit of fairness. After seven years of hard work he established in the Philippines a new record in diplomacy by winning the complete confidence of the natives. Said one man, "In all the Philippines there is no one so beloved for his gentle yet unrelenting manner, his absolute fairness and justice, as this soldier who had the unusual power of instilling love for himself and fear for his enmity at the same time."

In his boyhood his close friends report that this same quality often made him the protector of the younger boys when they were the victims of the school bully. "As a young fellow," states one of his early friends, "he was accommodating and never pushed himself forward. He was always ready to help other fellows who were not able to work out their problems. As a boy his decisions were always quick and accurate."

Of course the spirit of fairness implies the possession of a kindly nature as well as imagination. One cannot be fair or just to his enemies unless he can first get their points of view. This was the underlying quality in the work Lincoln did. He saw what his opponents saw but he also saw more. It is the quality which makes of a man or a boy "a good sport." He appreciates his antagonist and also—in the end —is appreciated by his antagonist.

A writer in the *Missouri Historical Review*, whose words have before been quoted, pays the following tribute to this quality in General Pershing:

With his scholarly attainments, his ability as a writer and speaker and his grasp of big problems, Pershing might have developed into a statesman; he certainly would have succeeded as a business man if he could have contented himself with the humdrum life in a downtown office; and with his attractive personality he might indeed have led a successful career as a politician, except for his unfortunate modesty which even in the army has frequently delayed for him a merited promotion. As a soldier, Pershing's methods are those of clemency rather than ruthlessness and he makes personal friends even of his enemies.

Writing as he did before the declaration of war with Germany he adds:

Since the death of General Funston he has been in command of the Department of the South, one of the important military posts of the country at the present time. With this country an active participant in the War of the Nations and the probability that a strong expeditionary force will be sent to coöperate with the Allies in France, what is more probable or desirable than that General Pershing should command it? He has participated in every war in which this country has been engaged for thirty years and in every campaign has added luster to his own name and distinction to American armies.

One has to read no more than the painstaking reports which he sent from the Philippines to the Adjutant General or to the Headquarters Department of Mindanao and Jolo to comprehend the mastery of details which has been a striking characteristic of General Pershing. From his recommendations concerning military posts and the disposition of the troops in the province he turns to deal specifically with detailed suggestions about cold storage plants and to present carefully prepared suggestions to aid the quartermaster from whom "too much is expected." It is easy for one to tell what *ought* to be done. The world has never lacked, nor does it lack now, multitudes of men who fancy they are competent to do that. But to find one who is able to tell how to do it—he is the individual for whom the world ever has a warm welcome. Many are officious, but only a few are competent or efficient.

Nor is this quality of mind and heart limited to details of administration alone. It applies also to his knowledge of men. The incident of the telegram to the former cook, John Kulolski, related in Chapter XVI, is illustrative. Most men find that for which they are looking. If they expect to find evil they seldom are disappointed. If their objective is the thing worth while, that too they find. To know men as well as maps, to study soldiers as well as supplies, to grasp the varying and differing elements that compose an army—these are the essential elements in a successful leader of men. To the German war lords their men may be merely "cannon fodder." To the public a French soldier may be a poilu, a British fighter a Tommy, an American a doughboy. To General Pershing every one that carries a gun is above all else a man. This is at once the basis of his confidence in and appeal to his followers. It may be because of this trait that Rowland Thomas and others have described General Pershing as "the most brilliant and most dependable general officer in our army."

Like many men who are large, physically as well as mentally, he has almost infinite patience. This quality too is so closely linked to self-control that at times it is difficult to distinguish between them. Confidence and self-possession are the foundation stones upon which patience rests. It is the man sure neither of himself nor of the goal he seeks nor of the cause for which he fights who becomes impatient. Was promotion delayed? Then he must wait with patience, first making himself fit to be promoted or doing his work in a manner that would compel recognition. Had the Moros for three centuries successfully resisted every attempt to subjugate them? Then his campaign must be so conducted that the little brown people must be made to see that the United States was seeking to help as well as to subdue. Had Germany for more than forty years been preparing armies to overthrow civilization and dominate the world? Then, "Germany can be beaten, Germany must be beaten, Germany will be beaten," is the quiet statement of the American Commander, because, having confidence in the cause for which he is fighting and faith in his fighters, he can be patient. With the end in view, there must be no hasty or impatient activity which might lead to disaster.

One distinguished writer on military topics

has called him the American Kitchener, because of his ability as an organizer. Points of resemblance there may be and doubtless are, and these are not limited to any one man, British or American, but the people of the United States are well content to take him as he is. If comparisons are to be made then the resemblance should be based upon the fact that the party to which reference is made is "like Pershing," not because General Pershing is like another.

It is a marvelous time in the history of the world and the times require men equal to the demand. Nearly four years of the war passed and up to that time the hearts of many were heavy because no one outstanding figure had appeared. The unspoken call was for a leader. Great men, good men and many of them were in evidence, but the Napoleonic leader had not appeared.

Then upon the insistence of the President of the United States a supreme commander, one brain, one heart, one sole power to direct, was found and the Allies were no longer separate

General Foch and General Pershing.

units, each free to come or go, without adhesion or cohesion. There was now to be one plan and one planner. The world already is aware of the result, for Foch has been tried and tested. The great unifying power has been discovered. The man for whom the world had been waiting had appeared and taken charge. Whether times make men or men make the times is a riddle as old as the one concerning the egg and the hen as to which was first produced. Without question both are true.

But no military genius can win battles, much less win a war, unless he is supported by strong men and true. And in the number of those who are closest to Foch is the Commander of the American Expeditionary Forces in France. All are rejoiced that he is where he is, but they are equally proud that he is what he is.

It is easy to paraphrase the words of the great Apostle to the Gentiles, and to say of General John Joseph Pershing that he too "is a citizen of no mean country." It is also easy to say that he is no mean citizen of that country, for he is both the citizen and the general, the man as well as the soldier. And there is the strongest possible desire on the part of his countrymen, that, upheld by his armies and helped by everyone in his native land, he may speedily add new luster to his name and to that of his own land until the words of the greatest orator of the new world may have an added significance and a deeper meaning—"I—I also—am an American!"

CHAPTER XX

HIS MILITARY RECORD

THE complete Military Record of General Pershing as it has been kept by the War Department of the United States is here presented. To the facts obtained from this Department are added a few later items, which the Acting Adjutant General kindly has provided.

JOHN J. PERSHING

BORN SEPTEMBER 13, 1860 IN AND APPOINTED FROM MISSOURI.

Cadet Military Academy....July	1,	1882
2nd Lt. 6th Cavalry.......July	1,	1886
1st Lt. 10th Cavalry.......Oct.	20,	1892
Captain, 1st Cavalry.......Feb.	2,	1901
Trs. to 15th Cavalry.......Aug.	20,	1901
Brigadier General.........Sept.	20,	1906
Accepted ....Sept.	20,	1906
Major General............Sept.	25,	1916
General ....Oct.	6,	1917

VOLUNTEER SERVICE

Maj. Chief Ord. Officer......Aug. 18, 1898
Honorably discharged.......May 12, 1899
Maj. A. A. G.............June 6, 1899
Honorably discharged.......June 30, 1901

SERVICE

Served with regiment on the frontier from September, 1886 to 1891; Professor of Military Science and Tactics at University of Nebraska, September, 1891 to October, 1895; was Instructor of Tactics at the Military Academy at West Point, N. Y., June, 1897 to May, 1898; served throughout the Santiago Campaign in Cuba, June to August, 1898; on duty in War Department, August, 1898 to September, 1899, when he left for Philippine Islands; served in Philippine Islands until 1903; member General Staff Corps 1903 to 1906; and also Military Attaché at Tokio, Japan; served again in Philippine Islands from 1906 to 1914; commanded Punitive Expedition in Mexico from March, 1916 to February, 1917; commanded Southern Department to May, 1917, and United States Forces in France since that date.

BATTLES AND CAMPAIGNS

Sioux Indian Campaign, South Dakota, September, 1890 to January, 1891; action near mouth of Little Grass Creek, South Dakota, January 1, 1891;

Las Quasimas, Cuba, June 24, 1898; San Juan, Cuba, July 1, 1898, and was recommended by his regimental commander for brevet commission for personal gallantry, untiring energy and faithfulness; and by the brevet board convened that year for the brevet of Captain for gallantry at Santiago de Cuba, July 1, 1898; in the field in Philippine Islands, November, 1900 to March, 1901, against General Capistrano, commander of insurrectionary forces; in command of an expedition against the hostile Moros of Maciu, starting from Camp Vicars, Mindanao, September 18, 1902; action at Gauan, September 18, and Bayabao, September 19, 1902; captured Fort Moro, September 29, 1902, driving the Moros from Maciu Peninsula on that date. He attacked the Moros at Maciu September 30, 1902, capturing their two forts, and returned to Camp Vicars, October 3, 1902; was in action at Bacolod, April 6 to 8, 1903; Calahui, April 9, 1903, and Taraca River, May 4, 1903. He commanded the first military force that ever encircled Lake Lanao; Punitive Expedition in Mexico, 1916 and 1917; and since June, 1917, commanding the Expeditionary Force in France.

An additional statement by the War Department:

John J. Pershing was appointed a Major General in the Regular Army, during a recess of the Senate, on September 25, 1916, with rank from that date.

His name was submitted to the Senate on December 15, 1916, for the permanent form of commission, in confirmation of his recess appointment, and the nomination was confirmed on December 16, 1916, the permanent commission being signed on December 20, 1916. He accepted his appointment as Major General on September 30, 1916.

He was appointed General on October 6, 1917, with rank from that date, for the period of the existing emergency, under the provisions of an Act of Congress approved October 6, 1917. He accepted this appointment on October 8, 1917.

Gen. Pershing sailed for Europe on May 28, 1917. Prior to that date a total of 211 officers and 919 enlisted men had embarked from the United States for Europe.

(1)

260

367)